1995

Marketing HRD Within Organizations

Jerry W. Gilley
Steven A. Eggland

Marketing HRD
Within
Organizations

Enhancing the Visibility, Effectiveness, and Credibility of Programs

Jossey-Bass Publishers · San Francisco

For sales outside the United States contact Maxwell/Macmillan International Publishing Group, 866 Third Avenue, New York, New York 10022

Printed on acid-free paper and manufactured in the United States of America

 The paper used in this book is acid-free and meets the State of California requirements for recycled paper (50 percent recycled waste, including 10 percent postconsumer waste), which are the strictest guidelines for recycled paper currently in use in the United States.

10% POST
CONSUMER
W A S T E

Library of Congress Cataloging-in-Publication Data

Gilley, Jerry W.
   Marketing HRD within organizations: enhancing the visibility, effectiveness, and credibility of programs / Jerry W. Gilley, Steven A. Eggland.
     p.   cm.—(The Jossey-Bass management series)
   Includes bibliographical references and index.
   ISBN 1-55542-402-3
   1. Personnel management—Marketing.   I. Eggland, Steven A.
   II. Title.   III. Series.
HF5549.G513   1992
658.3—dc 20   91-29615
                                  CIP

FIRST EDITION
HB Printing   10 9 8 7 6 5 4 3 2   *Code 9207*

The Jossey-Bass Management Series

Consulting Editors
Human Resources

Leonard Nadler
Zeace Nadler
College Park, Maryland

Contents

Preface

Several years ago, an important journal in the field of human resource development (HRD) reported that training budgets were among the first to be reduced during periods of economic decline. This practice greatly affects the human resources within an organization and seriously limits the organization's ability to compete.

Marketing HRD programs is not a substitute for quality and competence but a method of communicating the values of HRD to others. That, in essence, is the message of *Marketing HRD Within Organizations*. Marketing is a tool that can be used to improve the image, credibility, and acceptance of HRD, with the ultimate goal of integrating HRD into the fabric of the organization. If this is accomplished, HRD will become an equal partner with other essential components of the organization, such as finance, accounting, and operations.

Marketing for HRD programs also helps HRD practitioners to

- Focus attention on important market research before decisions are made
- Identify and rank target markets for HRD programs
- Base their programs on the identified needs and wants of their clients
- Develop appropriate goals and objectives
- Develop a promotional strategy that facilitates accomplishment of these goals and objectives

- Develop strategies for HRD programs and services, including cost-benefit and time/location analyses
- Develop proper selling techniques to inform and remind clients about the training programs and services offered by the HRD program
- Provide ways to manage and allocate human and financial resources
- Improve communication with other key members of the organization
- Publicize the accomplishments and results of HRD to other members of the organization

In the following chapters, we reveal how HRD practitioners can realize each of these aims. In addition, we examine ideas and steps that HRD practitioners can follow to design and implement a strategic marketing plan for their program.

Audience

This book is intended primarily for HRD practitioners who can influence the decision makers in their organization either directly or indirectly. That audience is large and diverse, for it includes not only HRD managers but instructional designers and internal consultants. At the same time, we hoped from the outset that all HRD practitioners could benefit from reading our book. After all, each HRD practitioner serves as an ambassador for the HRD program, and most if not all practitioners will some day be in a position to influence the key people in the organization. More broadly, then, *Marketing HRD Within Organizations* will appeal to anyone who is interested in improving the image, credibility, and effectiveness of HRD programs.

Importance of Strategic Marketing Planning

If HRD practitioners wish to achieve credibility, they must actively seek to convince management that they can improve the competitiveness and efficiency of the organization, further employee development, and effect behavioral change where necessary. We believe that the way to accomplish those objectives is to create and put into effect a *strategic marketing planning process* for HRD programs. Not only will strategic marketing planning improve the utility and perceived value of HRD programs, it will also help HRD practitioners identify marketing priorities, improve their planning and facilitation skills, and conduct internal analyses that will yield insight into the strengths and weaknesses of their programs. Simultaneously, strategic marketing planning will enhance familiarity with HRD among members of the organization.

Strategic marketing planning may also improve the ratio of opportunity costs associated with attending a training program to the benefits that attendance offers. It can assist HRD practitioners in identifying the factors that influence how clients select training programs and services and in appropriately responding to client demands and interests. But perhaps the chief reason that strategic marketing planning is so important to HRD is that it forces HRD practitioners to become directly accountable for their actions. If conducted properly, strategic marketing planning will help HRD practitioners communicate the value of their services to key members of any organization. Once this value is realized, organizational leaders as well as top management will be inclined to think favorably about budgets for HRD programs during economically depressed times. They will come to see that the programs help them accomplish their mission and objectives and ultimately improve the profitability and efficiency of the organization. We hope this book will contribute to those outcomes.

Overview of the Contents

This book has been designed to reveal how the strategic marketing planning process can be implemented by HRD practitioners. The first three chapters introduce the strategic marketing planning process and the following seven discuss the elements involved in implementing that process.

Chapters One through Three discuss the three critical components of successful strategic marketing planning: the marketing concept (Chapter One), the exchange process (Chapter Two), and the adoption process (Chapter Three). The first two of these are among the fundamental laws of marketing. The marketing concept itself requires HRD practitioners to place the needs of their clients before their own. It also requires HRD practitioners to design, develop, and implement training programs and services that help clients meet their performance and development needs. By adhering to the marketing concept, HRD practitioners will be able to resist the temptation to advocate favorite programs that do not clearly serve the interests of their clients.

The second component, the exchange process, is a transaction between two or more parties in which each offers something that the other perceives to be of value. HRD offers training programs and services to executives, managers, supervisors, and employees (clients) in exchange for their time, energy, effort, and personal commitment. A favorable exchange occurs when the training program or service offered by HRD is equal in value to the time, energy, effort, and personal commitment offered by the client. If, however, the client does not perceive the benefits as equal, the exchange will not occur or will be flawed. While this axiom appears simple, it is often overlooked by HRD practitioners.

Solid information is important to HRD practitioners in creating the most effective possible communications and promotional program, as well as in constructing the optimal product/service strategy. For this reason, the third component of the strategic marketing planning process, known as the adoption process, is critical to HRD because it reveals how clients select training programs and services. The adoption process consists of five separate but interrelated phases: awareness, interest, evaluation, trial, and adoption. This five-phase process also helps HRD practitioners identify their clients and reveals how clients react when they learn about a training program or service offered by HRD. It also takes into account individual differences and focuses attention on the different types of decision makers within the organization. This process allows HRD practitioners to develop promotional activities while increasing acceptance of training programs and services.

Building on the three components discussed in Chapters One through Three, HRD is ready to create the strategic marketing plan.

The plan comprises six distinct elements, each of which provides essential information for the HRD plan of action. In Chapters Four through Nine, we examine these six elements in detail:

1. Marketing mission: Why is marketing important?
2. Internal and external environmental analysis: What are the barriers and opportunities, the strengths and weaknesses, of the HRD program and its practitioners?
3. Marketing goals and objectives: Which outcomes is the marketing plan designed to produce?
4. Target audience and market research: What is the primary audience for HRD programs and how can this best be determined?
5. Marketing mix: How are the image and credibility of HRD going to be enhanced?
6. Marketing strategies: What is HRD's plan of action and how will the marketing plan be implemented?

In Chapter Four we discuss the marketing mission. Several fundamental questions that give the HRD practitioner a sense of purpose, direction, significance, and achievement are addressed in this context. A mission statement acts as an invisible hand to help widely scattered HRD practitioners work independently but cooperatively toward realizing the HRD program's goals and objectives. A marketing mission statement must, however, be motivational, realistic, and achievable in order to be useful. Simultaneously, it should be viewed by HRD practitioners as worthwhile and distinctive.

The second element in marketing planning, also discussed in Chapter Four, is an external and internal environmental analysis. This activity will assist HRD practitioners to determine which contingencies will help and which will hinder accomplishment of the HRD mission. The analysis will provide information needed to adjust for constraints and weaknesses while building on opportunities and strengths.

The next step in developing a strategic marketing plan is to identify marketing goals and objectives (Chapter Four), which will help provide a clear direction for the HRD program and aid in the measurement of the marketing plan.

Once the marketing goals and objectives have been identified, HRD practitioners will be ready to turn their attention to determining the most appropriate markets for training programs and services. In Chapter Five, three types of variables are identified that help HRD practitioners segment their marketing audience: behavioral, demographic, and geographic.

Although often overlooked by HRD practitioners, market research (also discussed in Chapter Five) is a prerequisite to creating a market segmentation strategy for an HRD program. Practitioners will begin their research by analyzing their market audience and dividing it into groups known as segments. From this analysis, practitioners can decide whether to try to serve all the segments or concentrate on the ones with the greatest potential. In this way, they can properly allocate the available financial and human resources.

The heart of strategic marketing planning is the marketing mix. Chapters Six, Seven, Eight, and Nine are devoted to discussion of this critical area. In Chapter Six, the marketing mix is defined as the blend of strategies that an HRD program uses to accomplish its goals and objectives. Chapter Seven discusses the crucial role pricing and location strategies play in formulating the marketing mix. Chapters Eight and Nine focus on helping HRD practitioners develop promotion strategies in order to effectively communicate the value of HRD both within the organization (Chapter Eight) and to clients (Chapter Nine).

In Chapter Ten, the reader will find sixteen action steps that HRD practitioners can take to construct and implement an effective strategic marketing plan.

Marketing HRD programs is a complex, holistic process made up of many steps and procedures, each designed to build upon the other. The primary outcome is a plan of action that should enhance the image and credibility of the HRD program and its practitioners. A secondary outcome is the creation of a responsive HRD program that anticipates changes and stands ready to revise its own mission, goals, objectives, and strategies, and the training programs and services it offers. The final result is an enhanced image, improved credibility, and greater effectiveness for HRD.

Lincoln, Nebraska   Jerry W. Gilley
November 1991   Steven A. Eggland

The Authors

Jerry W. Gilley is director of executive and professional development for William M. Mercer, Incorporated, a compensation, benefits, and human resources consulting firm, where he is responsible
for the design, development, and integration of HRD activities and
organizational development interventions. He received his M.A. degree (1983) from Louisiana Tech University in human relations and
supervision and his Ph.D. degree (1985) from Oklahoma State University in adult education and human resource development. His
current research interests include the professionalization of occupa-
tional fields and career development interventions.

Gilley works closely with senior executives and consultants in
their professional development activities. During the past five years,
he has written more than forty-five articles for professional and academic journals. He is the author of a monograph entitled *Professional Certification: Issues and Implications for Adult Education and
HRD* (1986, with Michael W. Galbraith) and of *Principles of Human
Resource Development* (1989, with Steven A. Eggland).

Gilley was formerly on the graduate faculty at the University
of Central Arkansas and the University of Nebraska, Lincoln. While
at the University of Nebraska he coordinated a master's and doctoral
program in human resource development.

Steven A. Eggland is professor of vocational and adult education
and human resource development at the University of Nebraska,

Lincoln. He received his B.A. (1966) and M.A. (1967) degrees from the University of Northern Iowa in business education with an emphasis in marketing. He holds a Ph.D. degree (1971) from the University of Wisconsin in curriculum instruction with a specialization in vocational education. He is a member of several professional organizations, including the American Vocational Association (of which he is national vice president for marketing education), the American Marketing Association (which named him Marketer of the Year for 1983), and the American Society for Training and Development.

Eggland's research interests include cooperative education, customer service, student-teacher interaction, and economic education. His books include *Introduction to Business, the Economy, and You* (1991, with A. Daughtrey, R. Ristou, and L. Dlaby) and *Communication That Works* (1992, with J. W. Williams).

Over the past twenty-five years, Eggland has taught marketing education, vocational education, and human resource development at various universities throughout the United States.

Marketing HRD Within Organizations

Chapter One

Why HRD Professionals Must Be Marketing Oriented

In 1977 Theodore Livitt wrote a classic article addressing what he called "marketing myopia." In it he revealed that every major industry was once a growth industry. However, as he pointed out, some industries continue to grow while others decline. "In every case the reason growth slowed or stopped," he stated, "is not because the market was saturated, [but] because there had been a failure of management to think strategically" (Barry, 1986). This same situation could face the field of human resource development (HRD).

Let us look at the value of strategic thinking for HRD. Such thinking can be defined as a process of systematically organizing the future, a process in which you utilize past experience as a filter for future decisions. It also allows you to consider the possible outcomes of your decisions or actions before implementing them. Strategic thinking can be used to identify the actions required to change the image of HRD as well as the opportunities available for HRD within an organization. It can also specify what an HRD program will achieve and what financial and human resources will be needed to accomplish it.

In reality, strategic thinking is more of a discipline than a process. HRD practitioners must develop the discipline to think about the future impact of HRD and react accordingly. This may require them to become "active" members of the organization's management team—to become proactive rather than reactive.

1

We believe that strategic thinking is a part of the marketing planning process. We will refer to it, then, as *strategic marketing planning*. For HRD it consists of six steps: (1) mission ("why"); (2) operational evaluation ("barriers"); (3) goals and objectives ("outcomes"); (4) target market ("who"); (5) marketing mix ("how"); (6) integration and implementation ("action"). These steps are outlined in Figure 1.1. Since they correspond to the plan of this book, let us take time to examine each one more closely.

Strategic marketing planning begins with the identification of an HRD *marketing mission statement*. This serves to provide HRD practitioners with a sense of purpose and direction. The statement should be compared to the organization's overall mission statement in order to determine if it reflects the organization's direction (see Chapter Four for more information).

Second, as an HRD practitioner, you should conduct an evaluation of the HRD program. This will provide you with information regarding the (external) opportunities and constraints that the program faces. The evaluation will also provide you with information regarding the (internal) strengths and weaknesses of the HRD program and practitioners. Analysis of this type is for determining which contingencies will help accomplish the marketing mission. It is often referred to as *internal/external environmental analysis*.

The third phase of strategic marketing planning is identifying the HRD program's marketing goals and objectives, which differ from the program's marketing mission. The marketing mission statement identifies where the program is coming from, while establishing goals and objectives identifies where the program is going, and so provides it with direction.

The goals and objectives are designed as a means of accomplishing the program's broader mission. If they fail to do this, you may discover that the HRD program is off course. As a result, you may be engaged in activities that do not enhance the image or position of HRD. (This phase, like the second one, is also covered in Chapter Four.)

The fourth phase (discussed in Chapter Five) is identification and analysis of the most appropriate participants for training programs and HRD services. From this analysis, it is possible to construct a comparison that will match programs with participants,

Figure 1.1. The Strategic Marketing Planning Process.

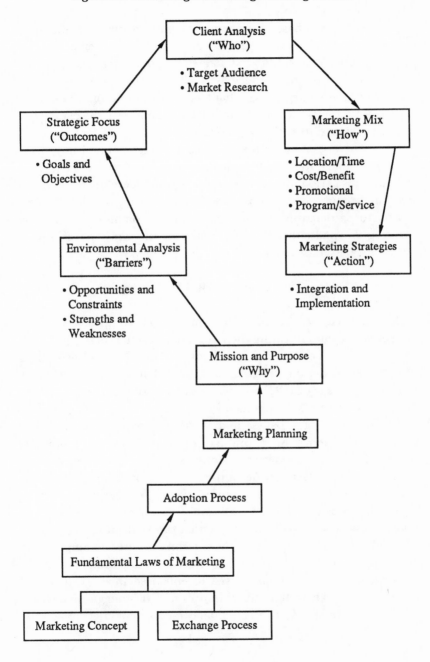

and so help you plan, utilize, and manage limited financial and human resources.

The next phase of strategic marketing planning is the most complex and difficult. It requires you to create and then apply one of four different *marketing strategies* for your program. They include product offering strategy (see Chapter Six); cost-benefit and location/time strategies (see Chapter Seven); and promotional strategy (see Chapters Eight and Nine). These combine to make up what is often referred to as the *marketing mix*.

The last phase of the strategic marketing planning process is one of integration and implementation (see Chapter Ten). It is during this period that specific approaches are developed regarding training programs, their cost-benefit relationship, and how to offer them to participants through promotional communication. It is during this phase that strategic marketing planning moves from a theoretical exercise to an action oriented reality.

The Nature of HRD Marketing

Marketing is not a substitute for quality and competence. It is a method of communicating the virtues of HRD to others within the organization. To that end, this book will develop and describe a seven-step model for strategic marketing planning, tailored to enhance the image of HRD within the organization.

Marketing has been identified as one of the primary reasons for the success of Japanese and Western European products and services in America. Marketing has, however, evolved to a point at which it is no longer viewed as simply selling or promoting a product, service, or idea for the purpose of improving its acceptance. While these activities are a part of marketing, marketing as a whole is viewed as a complex systematic and strategic process, designed to foster behavioral change in people that causes them to respond favorably. Therefore, marketing is a technique used to improve or enhance the image of products, services, or an organization. An important outcome of an improved or enhanced image will be increased acceptance. It is for this reason that strategic marketing planning should become an essential component of HRD programs.

Nevertheless, many people continue to think of marketing as synonymous with "selling." This can be a problem because selling is often considered negative; it reminds us of the time we were pressured into buying something we did not want or need. Such negative experience causes us to become suspicious and distrustful. We develop barriers to protect ourselves from being "sold" something that is not needed. Here is a very real example. Each of us receives thousands and thousands of pieces of promotional mail each year. For most of us, very little of it is read and even less is responded to. Why don't we open it up enthusiastically with great anticipation? The answer is simple. This type of mail represents little or nothing of value to us. We know that it is sent to thousands and thousands of people in the hope that 2 or 3 percent will respond. It is not focused on our needs or circumstances. As a result, we become conditioned to respond negatively to it. We have developed protective barriers against unsolicited mail, which we refer to as "junk mail." This type of technique causes us to regard all selling efforts as equally negative, including situations in which we are the sellers. This example illustrates many of our attitudes toward selling. But selling is only one small part of marketing. In fact, if marketing is conducted properly, the amount of selling should be significantly reduced.

What, then, is marketing, and what are its laws? HRD marketing can be defined as the offering of training programs and services that are designed to bring about voluntary exchanges of value with members of the organization (Gilley and Eggland, 1989). Implicit in this definition is the belief that training programs and services must be designed, developed, and delivered to bring about improved employee performance, satisfied developmental needs, and, as a result, greater organizational efficiency. Such achievements are then communicated to organizational leaders through promotional communications. The hoped-for outcome of these efforts is an improved image of HRD.

In order for marketing to be successful, HRD practitioners must adhere to two fundamental laws of marketing: the marketing concept and the exchange process.

The Marketing Concept: A Process of Client Satisfaction

The first law of marketing is the *marketing concept*. In HRD it can be defined as the improvement of performance deficiencies and the satisfaction of developmental needs of clients through HRD interventions. HRD interventions include training programs and HRD services. Clients are the people who benefit from the training programs, career development activities, and other services provided by HRD practitioners. This group includes employees, managers, supervisors, and executives. The organization is an indirect client of HRD because it is the ultimate benefactor of the clients' increased knowledge, skills, or improved behavior.

HRD practitioners who direct all their efforts at satisfying their clients are practicing the marketing concept. From this orientation, marketing is not used to manipulate clients but is focused on identifying and addressing the performance problems and developmental needs of the clients and the organization. As a result, training programs and services will be designed and developed in accordance with the clients' expressed interests. This will assure that the HRD program is centered around real client problems and needs. If it is, the HRD program will be supported as well as defended by users during difficult economic periods because training programs and HRD services are viewed as essential and even vital to the organization and its members.

The marketing concept, however, cannot be applied unless the HRD practitioner develops a service-oriented attitude, that is, an attitude of considering the thoughts of others before developing training programs. In this way, the practitioner's "ego" will be better managed and controlled.

The Exchange Process

The second law of marketing—its central concept, many believe— is known as the *exchange process*. We define the exchange process as the offering of value to another party in return for something of value. In the case of HRD, training programs and services must be viewed by clients as at least equal in value to the time, energy, and personal commitment exchanged for them. If the benefits to be received from a training program are viewed as greater than or equal to the time, energy, or personal commitment required from its clients, an exchange will take place. If, however, the benefits of training are not viewed in this way, an exchange will not take place. While this is a simple concept, it is often overlooked by HRD practitioners as they strive to develop HRD programs. It is important to remember that the more positive exchanges that occur between the HRD program and its clients, the more favorably the program will be viewed.

In order for you to become professional marketers of your HRD program, you must become skilled at understanding, planning, and managing exchange. You will need to develop skills in several areas, including how to identify and understand the performance problems and developmental needs of clients; how to design a training program or service to meet clients' problems and needs; how to communicate the values of a training program to clients; and how to determine the correct time and place for training. Each of these skills will be addressed later in this book.

The Value of Marketing to HRD

Several additional questions regarding the value of marketing should be addressed here. The answers to each will help you evaluate the importance of marketing your HRD program.

Why do HRD programs fail?

It is often difficult to determine why HRD programs are successful in one situation and not in another. We believe that HRD programs fail because they are not based upon the needs of the organization. Jim and Dana Gaines Robinson provide insight into this idea. In their book *Training for Impact* (1989), they identify the link between operational results and the development of skills and knowledge. They conclude that performance effectiveness is greatly improved when HRD professionals determine the gap between desired and actual performance, and then identify the relationship between the desired operational results and the skills and knowledge required to accomplish them. They further conclude that very few HRD professionals perform such analysis. This finding supports our belief.

Another closely related idea is that HRD programs fail because they do not adjust to changing conditions and needs within the organization. Many organizations grow and expand rapidly. During this period, HRD programs are in great demand. As the organization matures and growth slows down, however, HRD programs often fail to recognize the reduction in demand for training programs and services. As a result, the HRD programs fail to reposition their efforts to meet changing conditions. The outcome is often a drastic reduction in the HRD budget. Not only training programs and services but human resources are cut back and the value and importance of HRD within the organization are greatly reduced. This creates an impediment to future HRD efforts.

Others contend that HRD programs fail due to a lack of purpose. Purpose is defined here as "direction" or "mission." Because of this perception, HRD programs are not considered as having a strategic focus and their credibility within the organization suffers. Therefore, HRD programs are viewed as being outside the mainstream of organizational operations.

Still others contend that HRD programs fail because HRD practitioners fail to properly represent the value of HRD to the organization. Because the contribution of HRD to the overall success of the organization is not clearly seen, HRD programs are prevented from establishing a distinctive, positive image in the organization.

Another perspective is that HRD programs fail to focus on measures of performance improvement. Thus HRD is viewed as "show-and-tell" rather than a means to improve performance and efficiency. When this happens, HRD programs miss an excellent opportunity to demonstrate their capabilities for improving performance.

Still others believe HRD programs fail because their practitioners are not viewed as vital and contributing members of the organizational team. Chuck Butter, director of human resources for LTV Corporation, believes that the role of HRD practitioners is highly visible within an organization. As a result, they have an opportunity to significantly influence the direction of an organization. He also believes that HRD practitioners who fail to develop and maintain credibility or who do not demonstrate an understanding of the organizational culture and its purpose will be discredited very quickly. This too impedes the future growth of HRD.

Some HRD programs fail because HRD practitioners design, develop, and implement training programs that do not improve employee performance or organizational effectiveness and profitability. Their failure is compounded when the practitioners totally disregard the different learning styles of the participants. HRD programs that are not performance based have a very difficult time demonstrating their value to the organization. They are therefore severely downsized during difficult economic periods or changing marketing conditions.

Another common error is the use of so-called traditional theoretical approaches when more practical methods are required. Such a policy clearly reveals that some HRD practitioners lack experience in practical approaches to learning and do not understand the importance of demonstrating sound business practices.

Regardless of the reasons HRD programs fail, each failure adversely affects the image and credibility of the field and its practitioners. Therefore, it is in the best interest of all HRD programs and practitioners to eliminate any such failure. Adopting a strategic marketing focus is one way of doing so. This statement is based upon the belief that a strategic marketing plan is designed for the following purposes:

- Client satisfaction: to address employees' performance problems and satisfy their developmental needs
- Adjustment: to help HRD programs adjust to changing conditions
- Mission: to help HRD practitioners identify a mission for their program
- Promotion: to help HRD practitioners develop promotional activities that communicate the values of HRD to organizational decision makers
- Programs: to help HRD practitioners design, develop, and deliver training programs that are performance based and needs focused
- Visibility: to enhance the visibility of HRD practitioners through promotional communications and personal selling efforts

- Preparation: to help HRD practitioners prepare themselves by considering the environment and culture of the organization before they implement training programs and services
- Self-appraisal: to practice self-appraisal by learning to identify the strengths and weaknesses of the HRD program
- Goals: to set appropriate goals for an HRD program by identifying both its opportunities and its constraints
- Resources: to make effective use of resources by creating the optimal number of training programs and HRD services

Each of these topics will be addressed in greater detail in later chapters.

What are the characteristics of successful HRD programs?

Several years ago, Clark (1979) identified the characteristics of successful organizations. They included

1. A clear definition of where the organization was going and how it was to get there
2. An ability to capitalize on expansion opportunities
3. An anticipation of cultural, technological, economic, and political influences in the organization's environment
4. A well-defined strategy for getting things accomplished
5. An aggressive leader whose leadership style and skills inspired enthusiasm and confidence throughout the organization

Each of these characteristics should be adopted by HRD practitioners to improve the image and acceptance of HRD. The process begins with the development of leaders who inspire enthusiasm and confidence. It is clear that the HRD programs with leaders who inspire confidence, anticipate environmental changes, have a defined and defendable mission, a well-thought-out strategy for accomplishing that mission, and a flexible and adaptive approach to meeting clients' needs will succeed. On the other hand, HRD programs that are inflexible, rigid, reactive, slow to respond to changing conditions, and not based on clients' needs will fail or have their budgets cut drastically during difficult economic periods (Gordon, 1987).

One way of developing these five characteristics of a successful HRD program is through a strategic marketing plan as follows:

Characteristics of Program	*Strategic Marketing*
1. Clear definition	Mission statement
2. Expansion opportunities	Environmental analysis
3. Anticipation of environmental influences	Environmental analysis
4. Well-designed strategy	Creation of marketing strategies
5. Leaders who inspire enthusiasm and confidence	Application of marketing plan

It is strategic marketing planning that accounts for each of these characteristics of successful HRD programs. Therefore, such an approach can benefit HRD practitioners and programs greatly.

Why is marketing important for HRD?

It could be said that marketing-oriented HRD programs are ones that respond to the needs and wants of their clients. HRD practitioners in such organizations make every effort to identify clients' performance problems and satisfy clients' developmental needs. As a result, clients of marketing-oriented HRD programs may report higher levels of satisfaction with HRD. They are also more likely to communicate their satisfaction to others within the organization. Over time, such behavior can improve the image of HRD. This will make it easier for the HRD programs to attract even more clients to participate in training programs and HRD services. It should also help HRD practitioners understand that it is the HRD program's image that employees respond to. (Please understand that the closer the image of HRD is to reality, the better satisfied clients will be with HRD.) Employees who hold a positive image of HRD will be drawn to it, while those maintaining a negative image will avoid it. The bottom line is that perception becomes reality. This is one of the principal reasons why marketing is essential to HRD.

A second reason marketing is important to HRD is centered around the issue of credibility. Many HRD programs are viewed as outside the organizational mainstream. Thus they are not considered an integral part of the organization. In this situation, HRD is often viewed by employees and management as mere "overhead." In addition, many HRD practitioners fail to demonstrate their understanding of the organization's purpose and culture. In combination, these biases produce low credibility. Ultimately, the result is a negative image of HRD. Marketing-oriented HRD practitioners, by contrast, have a strong interest in how their clients perceive them and their training programs and services. Therefore, HRD practitioners must demonstrate their professional expertise as well as their understanding of organizational operations and culture. In this way they will help the HRD program to gain and maintain credibility.

Since the image of an HRD program is so critical to its acceptance, we feel it is essential to examine the concept more closely. We must first define the concept of *image*. Next, we will provide several suggestions on how to proceed in developing an improved image of HRD.

Image can be defined as the sum of beliefs, attitudes, impressions, and feelings that a person has toward an object or thing. Image can be measured either by *awareness* or by *favorability* (Barich and Kotler, 1991). Awareness refers to how aware clients are of the training programs and services provided by HRD. Favorability refers to the intensity of feelings clients have toward HRD and its interventions. In order to obtain an accurate understanding of the image of HRD, these two elements must be used in combination. Figure 1.2 reflects this relationship. Each location within this model reveals different implications for your HRD program as well as the action you must undertake in order to improve its image.

It is important to remember that an HRD program does not develop a positive image simply by running a public relations program. Rather, its image is a function of its competence as well as of its communications efforts. In other words, a positive image results when an HRD program creates real satisfaction for its clients and lets other essential decision makers know about it.

On the next few pages we will examine four different types of HRD programs, which vary in their familiarity and their favor-

Figure 1.2. HRD Program Image: Modeling the Dimensions.

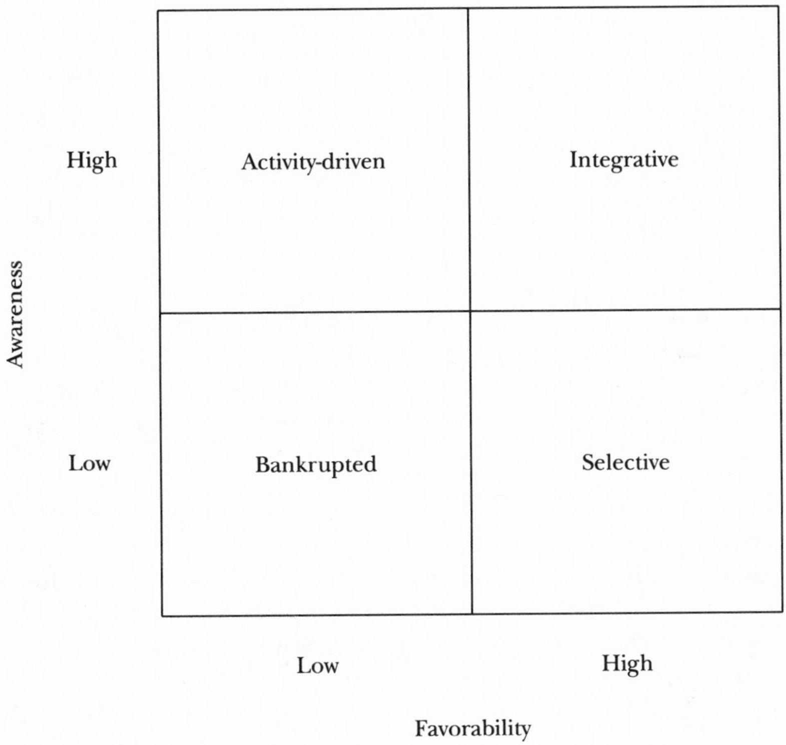

High	Activity-driven	Integrative
Low	Bankrupted	Selective

(left axis: Awareness; bottom axis: Favorability, Low — High)

ability rating. They include integrative, selective, activity-driven, and bankrupted HRD.

Integrative HRD. This type of HRD program is perceived by employees as highly favorable and a large number of employees are aware of the training programs and services offered. The program's image is very good and marketing efforts should be employed to maintain it. Such a program is highly useful to its clients and HRD practitioners communicate this value well.

It might be tempting not to market an integrative HRD program. However, marketing is important even to this type of program because familiarity can change as new employees are hired. In this situation a promotional strategy is most imperative. (This topic will be addressed in detail in Chapters Eight and Nine.)

Selective HRD. This type of program exists when HRD is used to accomplish specialized learning or is offered to only a select few employees. The image is positive either way, but only for those individuals who have had the opportunity to participate in the training program or use its services. The marketing effort in this situation is one of the most difficult, because most clients are unfamiliar with the program's value and importance. For this reason, you must communicate the value of HRD without the benefit of client involvement. Here, a strategic marketing approach is very much needed; it allows you to identify the mission of HRD, with its goals and objectives, and to select actions designed to enhance the image of the HRD program. The majority of this book is dedicated to this topic and will provide insight into the process.

Activity-Driven HRD. Most HRD programs fall under this category. It is not uncommon for an HRD program to maintain a library of training programs. A very large HRD program may have more than two thousand separate training programs available to employees. The problem with activity-driven HRD programs is not promotional communications but how to prioritize training programs and manage limited resources. A program strategy is most appropriate for this type of organization. This will enable you to identify which training programs are essential and which employees should use them (see Chapter Six for more information). An HRD program in this category must also consider why its favorability rating is not higher. The quality of each training program and service offered should be examined. It may also be important to examine the qualifications and skills of the HRD staff to determine their level of competence. Additional professional development may be required in order to enhance their knowledge and skills to an acceptable level.

Bankrupted HRD. This type of HRD program is not perceived as highly favorable by members of the organization. In addition, only a few members of the organization are aware of the HRD program or its offerings. Having its negative image shared by only a few people in the organization could be an advantage to the program. However, if the poor favorability rating is allowed to continue, more and more clients will become aware of the program's inadequacies.

In this situation, marketing should be used to help HRD practitioners in several ways. First, it should help practitioners develop an understanding of the marketing concept. This will enable them to develop training programs and HRD services that are centered around their clients' performance problems and developmental needs. A focus on client satisfaction will greatly help improve the favorability rating of bankrupted HRD programs. A second essential step for this type of HRD program would be the development of marketing skills for current HRD practitioners, who must develop a basic awareness of marketing before engaging in a complex and detailed marketing strategy. For example, the Dayton-Hudson Corporation, a Fortune 500 retailing organization, has maintained a unique promotional policy for all its retail outlets and subsidiaries. The policy states that each "store" must meet corporate standards before any promotional advertising campaign can be introduced. In other words, a spring housecleaning must be done before money can be spent on promotion or advertising. The same idea can be applied to the practitioners of this type of HRD. It is essential that they get their professional act together before concerning themselves with promoting the HRD program.

When is marketing appropriate for HRD programs?

If strategic marketing is a technique designed to enhance the image and credibility of HRD then it is essential to know under which conditions strategic marketing is best used. An answer to this question would help HRD practitioners better focus their marketing efforts and also make those efforts more effective. Of all the relevant conditions, eight are particularly important.

1. Strategic marketing is most appropriate when the image of the HRD program and its practitioners is unclear, diffuse, distorted, or misunderstood. This condition often becomes evident when the HRD program's budget shows major fluctuation. A history of such up-and-down budget adjustments may indicate that management is uncertain as to the role of HRD and its practition-

ers. Another sign of a negative image is when managers and employees do not view HRD as essential to the advancement of the organization and its mission. A third sign is when the salaries of HRD practitioners begin to decline in relationship to those of other employees. Finally, when other departments within the organization are becoming increasingly responsible for the design, development, and delivery of training programs, then HRD is in a poor state.

2. Strategic marketing becomes critical when the impacts of the HRD program cannot be identified. This is most common when HRD practitioners have not conducted cost-benefit analyses of their training programs and services. It is important to remember that a strategic marketing effort is less effective after management has begun to question the effectiveness of HRD. Management will view such an effort as hostile, defensive, and self-serving. Strategic marketing should be a proactive rather than reactive approach.

3. HRD practitioners should consider the economic condition of the organization and its industry. Strategic marketing of HRD has little impact when an organization is experiencing an economic downturn. Survival is then the watchword of the day. One method of reducing the negative impact on HRD during such periods is to demonstrate the value of HRD for the organization's profitability. Either a cost-benefit approach or results evaluations will do this admirably, but they must be conducted and communicated to upper management several quarters before the economic difficulty arises.

4. When training programs and services are not based upon the performance problems and developmental needs of the organization and its employees, HRD programs are in serious trouble. Strategic marketing is designed to help HRD practitioners combat this problem. The primary purpose of strategic marketing is to provide an approach that increases client satisfaction. As we have seen, the marketing concept and the exchange process are two examples of how strategic marketing can help HRD practitioners accomplish this purpose.

5. When HRD practitioners cannot identify the most appropriate markets for their training programs and services, strategic marketing becomes essential. This condition is best addressed by

implementing a program strategy outlined in Chapter Six. A closely related condition occurs when training programs experience declining or faltering demand. When this begins, HRD practitioners should examine the demand state of the training program and implement one of the appropriate marketing responses described in Chapter Two.

6. Strategic marketing is also appropriate when HRD training programs go unnoticed. Under such conditions, a promotional communications strategy is critical. This type of strategy is discussed in detail in Chapters Eight and Nine.

7. When an organization has recently been merged or acquired and/or a change in upper management has occurred, it is very important to communicate the utility of HRD. At this time, strategic marketing becomes vital. The six-step process outlined in the opening section of this chapter should be implemented. Remember, HRD is competing for limited resources. It is the HRD practitioner's responsibility to acquire an appropriate level of funding and support.

8. Organizational culture often shifts or changes. Today, many organizations are focusing on productivity and total quality management as a way of competing. HRD and its practitioners must understand such shifts and changes and adapt their programs accordingly. They must then communicate how HRD enables the organization to obtain its new cultural thrust. Strategic marketing allows HRD practitioners to examine their entire program and its offerings. It provides them with a systematic and strategic approach to getting things done—an approach that is essential in today's organization.

If one of these conditions exists or several of them exist in combination, a strategic marketing approach may be appropriate. Next, let us turn our attention to the arguments for and against strategic marketing.

What are the benefits and risks of strategic marketing?

Strategic marketing is very important to HRD programs because of the values it provides. However, marketing may cause some HRD practitioners to question its long-term effectiveness. As a result, the benefits and risks of marketing should be closely examined before adopting or implementing it.

Benefits of Marketing. Marketing can make a number of significant contributions to HRD programs. We have identified seven in this section.

1. Better communication with clients. Marketing provides HRD practitioners with an efficient communication system that informs potential clients about the availability of training programs and services. This type of communication system is essential to improving the familiarity of HRD within an organization. Such a system also helps HRD practitioners conduct critical need assessments and research for the organization.

2. Accent on client needs. Marketing forces HRD practitioners to consider the needs of their clients before offering them training programs and services. It does this by leading them to develop an HRD marketing mission statement, to establish goals and objectives, to execute a comprehensive and thorough program/service analysis, and to select appropriate marketing strategies. Some of these needs that you should consider are the right time of day to offer the training program, the most appropriate type of delivery system, the amount of time available for training, the personal and physical needs of participants, the background and experience of the participants, where training can be located, and which follow-up activities will foster learning transfer.

3. Better results, greater demand. Marketing helps create greater demand for training programs and services. As the need for HRD programs and services increases, more and more employees have an opportunity to benefit. The acquired knowledge or skill helps the organization become more productive, efficient, and profitable. Thus marketing of HRD, by helping the organization obtain its operational results, enhances the image of HRD within the organization.

4. Higher favorability. Marketing is a tool that HRD practitioners can use to communicate the impacts of HRD to other members of the organization. In this case, marketing is focused on improving the favorability of HRD within the organization. HRD

programs and practitioners that help an organization realize improved productivity, efficiency, and profitability should be recognized and rewarded. Through the promotional communication activities outlined in Chapters Eight and Nine, HRD programs and practitioners can improve their respective favorability ratings.

5. Management of change. Marketing is a means of addressing various demand states facing HRD programs. Demand is not a constant. Over time demand will change for every training program and service offered by HRD. HRD practitioners must know how to identify changing conditions and how to react. Marketing will provide the knowledge required to efficiently affect, alter, and improve demand for training programs and services. In Chapter Two, we will show how to identify several different demand states HRD practitioners are likely to face and how they should respond.

6. Management of resources. Marketing can be viewed as a strategic approach to the management and distribution of limited financial and human resources. In other words, marketing helps HRD practitioners decide which training programs and services are of highest value and will have the greatest impact on the organization. Having decided, they are in a better position to appropriate the needed funds or human resources. In simple terms, strategic marketing is a resource allocation tool designed to foster improved results.

7. Increased benefits for all. The contributions of strategic marketing can be summarized in terms of economic utility (Barry, 1986). This refers to the economic enhancement of an organization. Strategic marketing is designed to help HRD practitioners provide training programs and services to clients (organizational members) when they want them, where they want them, and in a way that encourages their enthusiastic involvement. As this cycle continues, the HRD program and its practitioners, the employees, management, and the organization itself all receive increased benefits. The exchange process is complete and all parties have increased their personal and professional value.

Risks of Marketing.

1. Wastefulness. Marketing is sometimes viewed as being wasteful—an example of such waste is encouraging additional train-

ing even after employees have developed a high level of competence. HRD practitioners with this type of motive will negatively impact HRD. It is simply an incorrect behavior. Likewise, simply increasing the number of employees who engage in training has little or no effect on productivity, efficiency, or profitability. While such actions may look impressive, they do not improve the organization.

2. Phantom results. Some HRD practitioners claim results or improvements that really do not exist. For example, an HRD practitioner may claim that a training program will increase employee productivity by 20 percent when there is no empirical evidence to support the claim. The same person may exacerbate the blunder by communicating this claim to upper management. Of course, such unsubstantiated claims seriously hurt the credibility of HRD and reduce its effectiveness in the future.

3. Overpersuasion. Marketing is such a powerful communication tool that it may create unnecessary needs and wants for training programs and HRD services in an organization. If this situation exists, then there could be a negative backlash, which could seriously hurt the credibility of HRD and its future effectiveness. Therefore, the strategic marketing of HRD must be balanced against the real needs and problems facing the organization.

What is the role of strategic marketing in HRD?

The best way to address this question is to examine the various orientations that HRD programs can have in trying to accomplish their mission. They include production orientation, product orientation, sales orientation, and market orientation. We will examine each in detail.

Production Orientation. Many HRD practitioners focus their attention on developing as many training programs and services as possible. Since their primary concern is to generate as much "activity" as possible, they give little thought to the real needs of the employees or the organization. They do this primarily as a way of justifying their existence. We refer to this approach as the "body count" method of HRD credibility. When this orientation is used, much attention is given to the efforts made by HRD practitioners to provide a large quantity of training programs and services. Little attention, however, is given to acquiring or using new knowledge and skills. HRD practitioners with this orientation are considered reactive. A reactive attitude often causes practitioners to respond to management's requests for training without analyzing the need for it or its importance. In summary, the production orientation emphasizes not quality outcomes but the number of training programs offered and the number of attendees that participate each year.

Product Orientation. Many HRD practitioners are in love with their training programs and services; they believe strongly in the value of what they contribute. This is certainly an appropriate attitude. However, their passion for their product can become a detriment to HRD. This is because a product orientation often causes HRD practitioners to resist any effort to modify current training programs and services regardless of how employees and management react. Practitioners who maintain this orientation demonstrate little interest in improving performance or satisfying others' developmental needs. In many cases, employees are "required" to participate in predetermined and selected courses. Their background, experience, and competence level are not considered important. This orientation is fostered by HRD practitioners because they consider themselves performance experts. They believe that others in the organization lack the skills, abilities, and academic preparation to recommend training interventions.

Sales Orientation. A few HRD practitioners maintain that their primary purpose is to stimulate interest in training programs and services. Their principal effort is therefore to get the "good word" out to as many potential clients as possible so that they will participate in training programs or utilize services. This effort is often a substitute for designing programs and services that meet the needs of the employees. Nevertheless, the HRD practitioners who use this approach believe that the effectiveness of HRD is directly linked to the time, energy, and money spent in promoting it.

Marketing Orientation. Some HRD practitioners have discovered the value of directing their attention to satisfying their clients. They hold that the primary purpose of HRD is to identify the performance problems and developmental needs of employees, managers, supervisors, and executives, and to satisfy them through the design, development, and delivery of appropriate training programs and services.

Kotler (1986) refers to the marketing orientation as "customer-centeredness." In other words, HRD practitioners direct their attention to increasing client satisfaction. In addition, HRD practitioners must understand that they are working for their clients. A client-oriented approach—a genuine interest in improving the performance and satisfying the needs of managers, supervisors, executives and other employees—will demonstrate this intent. In a marketing-oriented HRD program, the HRD practitioners will function as a team to improve client satisfaction. This type of behavior can also serve as an example for other departments within the organization.

The orientation of HRD practitioners greatly affects the way in which they operate with clients. The role of marketing in HRD is inevitably enhanced through the adoption of a marketing orientation. Under this condition, HRD practitioners focus their efforts on improving their clients' performance and satisfying their developmental needs. In so doing, they demonstrate their understanding of the two fundamental laws of marketing: the marketing concept and the exchange process.

What are the obstacles to strategic marketing planning in HRD?

There are several major obstacles to the strategic marketing planning of HRD programs. Each obstacle affects practitioners' attitudes toward the planning process. In addition, each one affects how marketing is utilized and integrated into HRD. In order for an HRD program to become marketing oriented, each of the following obstacles must be addressed:

Lack of Long-Term Commitment. HRD practitioners may feel that the immediate impact of marketing does not justify its initial costs in terms of resource allocation. However, it is not enough to understand the cost of marketing; HRD practitioners must also be committed to it as a process for effecting change over the long term.

Only then will they realize the benefits that strategic marketing can provide.

Lack of Needed Information. Strategic marketing planning relies on adequate and accurate information. This is perhaps its most vital aspect. HRD practitioners may not maintain or have access to the type of information required for appropriate decision making and planning. They also may not be able to interpret the information correctly. This will cause them to draw inappropriate conclusions from it.

Lack of Forecasting Skills. Accurate forecasts of future events and actions are essential if strategic marketing planning is to be effective. Many HRD practitioners may lack these skills. If this is the case, the desired outcomes of marketing may not take place. In fact, the HRD program could be hurt by the application of marketing.

Time and Priorities. HRD practitioners may not have the time to adequately develop a strategic marketing plan. Many believe that the time required to develop one could be used for other planning activities related to HRD. This is often a problem for those HRD practitioners who have never developed and implemented a process designed to produce long-term results.

Inadequate HRD Practitioners. It would be naive to believe that all HRD practitioners are competent enough to contribute to the process of marketing planning. While many are able to make an immediate and significant contribution, many simply lack the necessary skills. If an HRD program does not have available the qualified human resources for developing and implementing a strategic marketing plan, it should not try to implement one until it has acquired them.

Lack of Appropriate Planning Procedures. Some HRD practitioners fail to implement planning procedures for their program. As a result, much of the information required for an effective strategic marketing plan is not accounted for or is improperly labeled. It would be a waste of time and effort to develop a strategic marketing plan without first constructing a process for adequate data collection.

Tunnel Vision and Limited Forecasting Skills. Too many HRD practitioners rely only on the past to determine future action for their program. Such narrow-mindedness leads to their developing plans that are merely reactionary or are copies of last year's plans. Organizations evolve so quickly today, this obstacle is one that HRD practitioners must overcome if they ever hope to develop and implement a strategic marketing plan.

Conclusion

Marketing can be a mechanism that enables HRD programs to succeed. The process of marketing planning enables HRD practitioners to inspire enthusiasm and confidence because it is a process designed to improve long-term results. It is based upon a clearly defined mission. It accounts for various environmental influences that have an impact on the program. It is based upon the performance problems and developmental needs of the clients. It builds on the strengths of the HRD program and is directed at the development and enhancement of a clear, positive image of HRD within the organization.

Peters and Waterman (1982) have identified eight common attributes of successful organizations. One of these is a close relationship with clients. We believe that this is an attribute HRD practitioners must develop. They must be willing to get to know those they serve and learn from them. Strategic marketing is a process that enables this to occur because it is based upon the performance problems and developmental needs of HRD clients and not upon the needs of HRD practitioners.

The authors (Gilley and Eggland, 1989) have identified several implications for HRD programs and practitioners regarding the strategic marketing planning of HRD.

1. A strategic marketing plan can benefit an HRD program by focusing upon the needs of its ultimate users.
2. A strategic marketing plan is beneficial because it increases

HRD practitioners' awareness of the importance of the exchange process.

3. A strategic marketing plan is helpful because it forces HRD practitioners to go through a systematic rethinking process designed to help refocus the HRD program.

4. A strategic marketing plan forces HRD practitioners to analyze their user groups in order to determine the most appropriate markets for training programs and services.

5. A strategic marketing plan will help HRD practitioners determine the most appropriate blend of marketing variables needed to enhance the image of the program.

6. The establishment of a marketing strategy is a means for bringing together both the clients and the HRD program in such a way as to establish an overall strategic approach for the program.

7. A strategic marketing plan is a holistic approach, designed to improve the image of the HRD program throughout the organization.

Chapter Two

Placing the Organization's Needs First: Meeting Expectations for HRD

In Chapter One we identified two fundamental laws of marketing: the marketing concept and the exchange process. These two laws are so critical to the success of strategic marketing that a comprehensive review of each is necessary.

The Marketing Concept Revisited

As we saw in the previous chapter, the marketing concept means that HRD practitioners direct their efforts at improving the performance and satisfying the developmental needs of the client group— the organization's executives, managers, supervisors, and employees. HRD practitioners who adopt the marketing concept approach find effective and efficient means of serving their clients without manipulating them. They accomplish this by providing the types of training programs and services that improve performance and satisfy developmental needs. The idea appears to be both simple and straightforward, but it is often misunderstood, forgotten, or overlooked. In order to develop the marketing concept, HRD practitioners must create an information gathering system. Such a system should include formal and informal needs assessments, focus group activities, and client interviews.

It may also be important to interview managers and supervisors. This will allow HRD practitioners to identify the performance problems and developmental needs of their clients. Once they have been identified, HRD practitioners should use this information as the basis for designing and developing all training programs and services.

An information system designed to gather critical client information is usually very expensive. As a result, HRD practitioners must be willing to commit a substantial portion of their HRD budgets to its development and maintenance. But without an adequate information system, an HRD program cannot be problem and need focused. In other words, the program cannot be client oriented.

HRD practitioners must also be dedicated to implementing training programs and services that improve performance and satisfy developmental needs. The HRD program will then be certain to have a positive impact on the organization. Such a results-oriented approach requires an organization-wide evaluation strategy that measures the impact of HRD. Practitioners must design, develop, and implement this evaluation strategy. Once employed, a results/impact evaluation strategy can be used to enhance the image of HRD and its practitioners. If the results are properly communicated to upper management, such a strategy will further improve management's perception of HRD.

Finally, as an assurance that their services are of professional quality, HRD practitioners must be willing to be held accountable to clients. In this way they will also communicate to organizational leaders the commitment they have to quality and improved performance.

HRD practitioners who adopt the marketing concept are not doing so at the expense of their program's goals and objectives. Rather, they are adopting it to further the mission of HRD by providing the types of training programs and services that are valued by executives, managers, supervisors, and employees for their effectiveness. It is this that results in client satisfaction.

The Exchange Process Revisited

The exchange process calls for the offering of value to another party in return for equal or greater value. This is a simple concept in principle. In actual practice, however, the exchange process is much more complex. Here, the components that make up the exchange process will be examined. They include the basic requirements that must be met before exchange can occur, the five different types of benefits received from an exchange, the two different types of exchanges, and the different methods of evaluating the exchange process.

What are the requirements needed in HRD for exchange to occur?

Barry (1986) has identified two basic requirements of exchange: there must be two parties actively seeking an exchange, and each party must offer something that the other perceives to be of value. If either party does not have something of value to exchange, the exchange will not take place. Each party will analyze the potential for exchange based upon the probability of receiving benefits. We will examine the different types of benefits later in this chapter.

Kotler (1986) has identified two additional requirements for exchange. First, each party must be capable of communicating with the other, which includes being able to describe what is being offered for exchange, its features, benefits, special characteristics, what form it will take, when, where, and how it will occur, and what must be exchanged for it. In HRD, an offering for exchange includes training programs and services. The most common items offered in exchange by clients are time, effort, and commitment to change.

The second additional requirement of exchange is that both parties are free to accept or reject the offer. This implies that no excessive pressure or coercion is present and both parties are engaging in voluntary behavior. Under these conditions, both parties will benefit from the exchange and receive something of value that they desire.

To better understand the concept of exchange it is best to view it as a process made up of smaller subsets rather than as a single event. It begins with sharing information or making introductions referred to as *interactions*. The complexity of the exchange will determine the number of interactions that occur. If both parties believe that they can benefit, the interaction(s) is/are said to have *exchange potential*. Next, the process moves to a stage where both parties try to find mutually agreeable terms for exchange. This is referred to as *negotiations*. When successfully completed, negotiations result in an activity known as a *transaction*, based upon mutually agreed terms of exchange. When negotiations are not successful, exchange does not take place.

What are the benefits of an exchange?

According to Lovelock and Weinberg (1984), benefits of exchange can be categorized in five groups:

1. Sensory benefits: the five senses of taste, smell, sound, feel, and appearance
2. Psychic benefits: sense of accomplishment or achievement
3. Place benefits: convenience, comfort, and attractiveness
4. Time benefits: speed and convenience
5. Monetary benefits: actual or potential financial reward or monetary gain

All five kinds of benefit can be received by clients through exchanges with HRD. In HRD, however, the most common types of benefit are psychic and monetary. Most clients will report a sense of accomplishment as a result of participating in a training program. This benefit becomes observable through improved performance and increased quality in products, services, and interpersonal interactions. Such an exchange results in increased organizational efficiency and profitability. Thus, the organization receives a monetary benefit.

What types of exchange are there and who benefits from them?

There are two types of exchange: two-way and three-way. Each will be examined separately and the benefactors of each type of exchange will be identified.

Two-Way Exchange. An exchange between two parties is known as a *two-way exchange*. In this situation, one party offers something of value to another party who offers something of value in return. As stated previously, exchange will occur when the value offered by one party is greater than or equal to the value offered by another party.

Figures 2.1 and 2.3 illustrate two different two-way exchanges in HRD. Each reveals what is actually being exchanged, its perceived value, and the result of the interaction between the two parties. Figure 2.1 indicates that many HRD practitioners operate as internal consultants to their organization. They provide a variety of counseling activities that are considered services. These may include needs assessments, conference planning, skills identification, change interventions, team building, cultural development, and performance analysis. Each of these activities requires many months to reveal its long-term effects. The value exchanged by internal consultants (here, the HRD practitioners) could include such observable and measurable characteristics as greater efficiency and productivity. They can also exchange intangible ones such as improved attitudes or greater cooperation.

The type of value being exchanged here must be carefully considered. HRD practitioners must examine the outcome of their intervention to determine if the results claimed can be accomplished. Once the value that is to be exchanged has been determined, it must be communicated to the identified audience. (We address the procedures for this type of communication in Chapters Eight and Nine.) The audience will examine the offer and determine if they are willing to exchange their time, effort, and commitment to change for it. Clients must be willing to participate in the process of analysis (that is, exchange time) and provide insights regarding the appropriateness of the various suggestions made by the HRD practitioners (that is, exchange effort). In addition, clients must be willing to implement the changes recommended by the HRD practitioners (exchange commitment). If both parties see value and benefit from the involvement, the exchange will occur.

During this interaction, HRD practitioners should continue to assure clients that the values offered can be achieved. As negotiations continue, clients will be weighing the costs of participating (time, effort, or commitment to change) against the value received (improved efficiency, greater productivity, improved attitudes). This process is known as the *value equation* (Figure 2.2). An exchange will occur only if the benefits of participating outweigh the costs.

Figure 2.1. The Two-Way Exchange Process: Services.

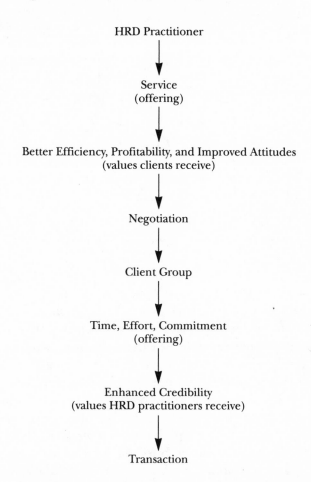

HRD Practitioner

Service
(offering)

Better Efficiency, Profitability, and Improved Attitudes
(values clients receive)

Negotiation

Client Group

Time, Effort, Commitment
(offering)

Enhanced Credibility
(values HRD practitioners receive)

Transaction

HRD practitioners must, however, consider the reputation of their programs when offering its claims of value. A positive relationship with clients will develop when positive exchanges occur, while negative exchanges will result in weakened or poor relationships. Therefore, practitioners should not make an offer to clients if they do not believe they can produce a positive exchange. A careful selection of offerings may be far more effective than providing a large number of services.

The second type of exchange that can occur between HRD

Figure 2.2. The Value Equation.

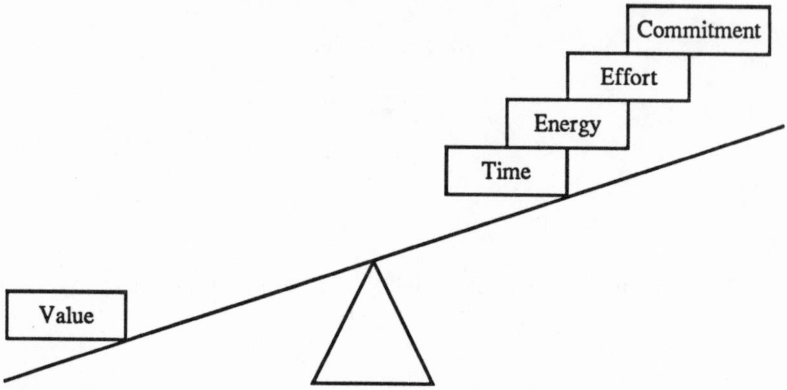

practitioners and their clients involves the offering of a training program to potential clients (Figure 2.3). Again, HRD practitioners must carefully consider the performance outcome desired. Having done so, they should create a list of performance objectives to serve as a guide in the design and development of the training program. These objectives should then be converted into persuasive language and communicated to potential clients as statements of value. Emphasis should be placed on the benefit that a person will receive by participating in the training program. The statements will also serve as the primary vehicle for negotiations with clients.

In terms of the value equation, clients must be willing to attend (time), to participate and engage in activities and role plays (effort), and to apply the concepts learned (commitment). For clients, the decision is based upon the perceived value of this type of exchange. Again, communication becomes an important tool in the exchange process. HRD practitioners must communicate the purpose, value, and impact of a training program as well as identify its long-range results. If HRD practitioners successfully represent and communicate the value of training programs, a transaction will occur. Exchange will take place and the credibility of HRD will be enhanced.

Three-Way Exchange. While two-way exchanges are the most common kind, multiparty exchanges exist in most HRD situations. Of

Figure 2.3. The Two-Way Exchange Process: Training Programs.

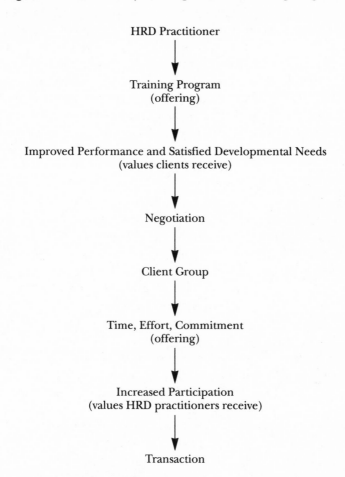

HRD Practitioner

Training Program
(offering)

Improved Performance and Satisfied Developmental Needs
(values clients receive)

Negotiation

Client Group

Time, Effort, Commitment
(offering)

Increased Participation
(values HRD practitioners receive)

Transaction

these, a three-way exchange is the most likely to occur. The primary reason is that the benefits received from training programs and HRD services affect the organization as well as the person participating. Thus the HRD program must provide training and services that not only improve performance but result in improved organizational effectiveness and profitability. If this occurs, the organization will be motivated to allow its employees to participate in future training programs and services. Support of this type reinforces and improves the image of HRD.

The types of interactions and negotiations are exactly the same in a three-way exchange as in a two-way exchange. This is because a three-way exchange consists of three two-way exchanges: between the organization and its employees, the employees and the HRD program, and the organization and the HRD program.

Three-way exchanges, however, become more complicated than two-way exchanges because an extra party is involved. In addition, the reaction of this extra party may impact the success of the exchange. Accordingly, HRD practitioners must be as concerned with the exchange between the employees and the organization as they are with the one between the HRD program and the employees.

As we discussed previously, exchange will not occur unless both parties receive something of value that is equal to or greater than the value they are offering to exchange. Therefore, in a three-way exchange a breakdown can occur between the HRD program and the employees, the HRD program and the organization, and the employees and the organization. If a three-way exchange is to be successful, HRD practitioners must become responsible for the management of each of these two-way exchanges.

Figure 2.4 illustrates a three-way exchange process resulting from the exchange of training programs and services offered by the Human Resource Development Department of Birkman and Associates, a management and human resources consulting firm in Houston, Texas. As you can see, each of the three parties receives different benefits from the exchange process. The success of this exchange will be based on the quality of exchange between each of the parties involved. We will now examine this exchange in greater detail in order to better understand the three-way process.

The Human Resource Development (HRD) Department is engaging in two two-way exchanges, one with the client group (consultants, technicians, managers, supervisors, and clerical workers) and the other with the organization (Birkman). The client group is also engaged in two two-way exchanges, with the HRD Department and Birkman. Simultaneously, Birkman is engaged in two two-way exchanges, with the client group and the HRD Department. In each and every one of these two-way exchanges, an equal exchange of value must take place. If this does not occur, the process will break down.

Figure 2.4. Three-Way Exchange at Birkman and Associates.

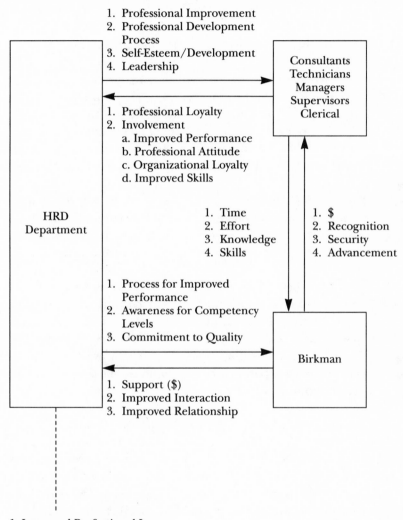

1. Improved Professional Image
2. Leadership Role Improved
3. Improved Involvement and Commitment on the Part of Membership
4. Improved Financial Support (employer's and members)
5. Identity of Employees Crystallized

Source: Birkman and Associates. Reprinted by permission.

The outcomes of a successful three-way exchange for the HRD Department are outlined at the bottom of Figure 2.4. It can benefit in any of five ways:

1. Improved professional image of the department and its prac-
    titioners
2. Improved leadership role within the organization, a develop-
    ment that will impact future decisions related to HRD
3. Improved involvement and commitment on the part of the
    client group regarding their personal and career development
4. Improved financial support from the organization for the de-
    sign, development, and implementation of future training pro-
    grams and services
5. Better understanding by employees of their respective roles
    within the organization and greater ability to identify potential
    career paths and developmental opportunities, all of which
    helps the E&T Department better target its future efforts

If each of these benefits is realized, the image of Birkman's HRD Department will be greatly enhanced. The credibility of the HRD practitioners within the department will also be improved. These positive outcomes will enable the department to expand its influence within the organization. Over time, it will even come to be viewed as an essential part of the organization—one that withstands the worst economic difficulty.

What obstacles and barriers affect the exchange process?

Exchange would be easy if people and organizations could always have a choice between two positive outcomes. Dealing with such a choice is known as making an *approach-approach decision.* However, decisions of this type can also cause conflict because they require people to decide between two equally desirable alternatives. For example, the choice might be between attending a training program on leadership development, which could greatly improve one's promotional opportunities, or going on vacation with one's family. Another example would be having to decide whether to participate in a career development workshop that could advance one's career, or complete a project that is valued by one's CEO. Both of these examples would have only positive outcomes, would be appropriate decisions either way, and would cause little stress. However, when one positive decision is placed in combination with another, the exchange process becomes very difficult.

While having to select between two positive outcomes is common, most decisions involve both positive and negative outcomes. These are known as *approach-avoidance decisions.* They appear to be easier to make because of the choice between positive and negative. Most decisions, however, involve negative outcomes that cannot be eliminated. In the exchange process, the positive value received must therefore be weighed against the negative outcomes. The value equation is again a model that can be used for this type of decision.

Let us provide an example. Not long ago William M. Mercer, Inc., the world's largest compensation, benefits, and human resources consulting firm, offered a strategic sales training program to its senior consultants in the New York region. It required extensive role playing and several follow-up activities, all of which was viewed by senior consultants as a negative. In addition, the course was to last three days, which would prevent consultants from performing their normal consulting activities. It is important to note that senior consultants commonly bill clients in excess of $350 per hour. This would mean that each consultant attending the twenty-four-hour program would lose about $7,400 of billable time. Therefore, the time spent participating in the program was seen as a negative. By participating, however, the consultants would develop sales techniques and skills tailored for the professional services marketplace. In addition, they would develop advanced interpersonal skills and techniques for working effectively with senior executives. These were seen as positive outcomes.

As you can see, the conflicting outcomes complicated the exchange process. The consultant had to be able to weigh the negative outcomes against the positive benefits and reach a decision. This is very difficult when the positive outcomes are not quantifiable.

HRD practitioners can help decision makers when they face such approach-avoidance situations. First, they must take the initiative by conducting quantitative impact and results evaluations that will support their claims of performance improvement. Second, HRD practitioners can assist by communicating the benefits of their training programs and services. This will help decision makers compare actual results with actual costs. Finally, HRD practitioners can point out to decision makers the dilemma that they are facing and provide assurances that the training program or service being considered is the best possible intervention.

Another type of decision that causes conflict is known as an *avoidance-avoidance* decision. This type of decision forces a person to choose between two or more negative outcomes. For example, many employees are asked to attend long, intense, and difficult training programs, hundreds of miles away from home, during the weekends, and without being relieved from their current work load or responsibilities. The employees are often not provided with any information regarding the value of the training program or how it will benefit them in their careers. They are simply instructed to attend a training program. Several negative outcomes are involved in this exchange. They include the long, intense, and difficult training activity; separation from family; the inconvenient time; the lack of relief from work load or responsibilities; and the paucity of information regarding the purpose or nature of the training. This type of decision causes the greatest amount of stress and often prevents positive exchange from occurring. The attitudes of participants are greatly affected by this type of decision.

Avoidance-avoidance decisions can be made very easily by clients. Under these conditions, the training programs offered are of little perceived value and are not supported by managers and program sponsors. In fact, participation is often viewed very negatively. Under these conditions, HRD practitioners must point out the benefits for their clients prior to their attendance. They must positively influence managers and supervisors who demonstrate little regard for training and manage the training process so that it does not interfere too much with employees' personal lives. HRD practitioners must also be sensitive to any unnecessary demands of training and provide realistic and practical applications of it for employees. Failure to address these issues will result in the weakening of HRD.

Are there different models of exchange that help HRD practitioners predict possible outcomes?

Kotler (1986) has identified three models that can be used to predict the outcomes of exchange situations: the economic model, the equity model, and the power model. The *economic model* maintains that people make decisions regarding exchange based on their self-interest. In other words, people select the alternatives that seem to be in their best interest. They examine situations by identifying the benefits and subtract the cost to arrive at personal net gain. They then compare various alternatives and select the one with the highest net gain. This model most resembles the value equation previously discussed.

The *equity model* maintains that two people reach an agreement regarding the exchange based upon what is fair to both parties. This approach emphasizes the importance of collaboration and shared mutual interest. The equity model is the only evaluation model that places importance on the relationship between the two or three parties involved in exchange.

The *power model* maintains that people seek to gain an advantage as a result of exchange. They will even exploit situations and exercise their power of position in an attempt to gain this advantage, a process often called "leveraging one's position." In this situation, fair exchange is often not possible. As a result, HRD practitioners must become very creative and persuasive in their attempts to neutralize more powerful people who desire to dominate the exchange process.

Demand for HRD and How to React to It

The needs of executives, managers, supervisors, and employees—of HRD clients, in short—manifest themselves as *demand*. Demand is a marketing term that indicates the number of people who have the capacity and willingness to exchange time, effort, and commitment for a training program or service offered by HRD practitioners. Demand can vary for each training program or service offered. We will address the different demand states later in this chapter.

HRD practitioners can respond to demand in one of three ways:

1. They can accept the client's demand and take action. This is often done without additional needs analysis or performance assessment.
2. They can refuse to address the client's demand.
3. They can react by conducting a comprehensive analysis of the situation and determining the performance problems and developmental needs of clients. They can then respond accordingly.

Let us provide an example that illustrates these three types of response. A department manager of a retail store requests that customer relations training be offered to the department's employees. What action can the HRD practitioners take? First, they can respond by designing, developing, and implementing a training program that addresses this perceived need. Although this reaction demonstrates the practitioners' willingness to solve problems as well as the service-oriented nature of HRD, two other conditions must be present for this response to be appropriate. First, the manager's perception of the problem must be accurate. This means that customer relations really is a serious problem that has affected employee performance and organizational results. The second condition is that a training program be designed that provides the knowledge and skills that will remedy the problem. If these conditions are met, then the response is correct. But what if the manager's perception of the situation is not correct? In that case, a reaction of this type by HRD practitioners can make an already bad situation worse.

Second, the HRD practitioners might refuse to react to the demand on the grounds that a training intervention could not adequately address the need. This response may be appropriate but falls short because it is not based on empirical evidence. It also does not demonstrate a client-centered approach.

Third, the HRD practitioners can act in a way that combines the first two responses, enabling them to be client centered by responding quickly to client problems and needs. It also allows them to respond only to problems and needs that are documented. This can be accomplished by their not responding to a client's demands until they have conducted an analysis of the situation and determined whether training is appropriate.

Such an analysis may range from the very formal to the very informal. Several factors help HRD practitioners determine the degree of formality. They include the type of training request, the situation within the organization, the time available for an analysis (which will depend on the seriousness of the problem or need), and the level of management requesting training. Once this has been determined, the results must be carefully communicated to the person(s) requesting the training program or service. It is certainly appropriate for HRD practitioners to refuse the client's requests if evidence cannot be found to support the problem or need.

Why is demand different for each HRD training program and service and how can HRD practitioners respond?

This two-part question is critical to the selection of appropriate marketing strategies. HRD practitioners must understand the characteristics of differing demand states and the correct marketing response for each one. But first, what are the factors that determine which demand state HRD practitioners will face?

Several different demand states exist in HRD because the interest in and need for training programs and services varies from organization to organization. In addition, the credibility of HRD is better in some organizations than others. Timing also affects the demand state of an organization. Both its financial condition and its cultural climate are relevant here. Employees' attitudes toward HRD can also affect the demand state, as can previous experience with HRD programs and services. No matter what its origin, each demand state requires a different marketing response. The task of HRD practitioners is to identify the state and then select an appropriate response. We have identified six different demand states that are appropriate for HRD. Each will be addressed in the following pages.

Negative Demand and Conversional Marketing. Many HRD programs face a negative demand situation. It is a state where most of the important clients maintain a negative perception of training programs or services offered by the HRD program. Some may even fully resist or avoid the training programs or services. As a result, the HRD program and its HRD practitioners are viewed as an overhead expense that should be managed or eliminated altogether.

Many things can cause this condition. The training programs may be poorly designed, developed, and/or implemented. In addition, they may not be based upon the performance problems and developmental needs of clients. The HRD practitioners may lack competence and professional identity. Clients may maintain a negative attitude toward learning or development activities in general. Upper management may be supportive of HRD, causing middle managers and supervisors to view it as a waste of time. The training programs and services provided may not be directed at improved productivity and employee performance, and a comprehensive evaluation strategy may not have been developed that could provide evidence of the value of HRD. HRD practitioners may lack understanding of the corporate mission and goals. A lack of communication with clients may have reduced the opportunity for HRD practitioners to demonstrate their value to the organization, or they may have failed to communicate the positive results obtained through increased knowledge, skills, or improved behavior. The practitioners may lack consulting and facilitation skills, as well as understanding of the cultural and political issues affecting the organization. Finally, the practitioners may have failed to demonstrate the cost-benefit relationship of training and HRD services.

Each of these factors may combine with one or more of the others to produce a poor image of HRD within organizations. These failures can also contribute to a negative image for the entire HRD field. Therefore, HRD practitioners must address the situation by developing a strategic marketing plan that reverses negative demand. This type of marketing response is known as *conversional marketing* (Kotler, 1987). It is one of the most challenging and difficult tasks that HRD practitioners will face.

The most critical step in conversional marketing is to discover why clients resist training programs and services. Such resistance can be identified through traditional research methods such as questionnaires, interviews, or focus groups. The focus group is often considered the best method for discovering why clients continue to resist HRD, because it helps HRD practitioners compare responses as well as measure the intensity of the responses. The focus group method is also an excellent way of altering clients' beliefs and attitudes regarding HRD. By using this face-to-face approach, HRD practitioners also have direct access to opinion leaders, to whom they can communicate the intent, purpose, and mission of HRD. As a result, focus group participants can become better acquainted with HRD practitioners and their approaches. Another outcome could be that the participants serve as spokespersons for the HRD program.

Once HRD practitioners have identified the reasons for negative demand, an analysis of the program's strengths and weaknesses should be conducted. This will serve as an internal audit of the HRD program and its practitioners. Building on the strengths and improving the weaknesses can improve the credibility of HRD. Other components of conversional marketing fall within the scope of the strategic marketing planning approach outlined in the remaining chapters of this book. Special emphasis should be placed on promotional strategies, and personal selling of HRD to clients should be the primary promotional activity used. This will enable HRD practitioners to communicate the virtues and values of HRD directly to clients (see Chapter Nine for more information).

No Demand and Stimulational Marketing. In this situation, clients are indifferent to or uninterested in the training programs and services offered by the HRD program. This is because HRD programs are perceived as providing little value to the organization. If this type of demand state is allowed to continue, it may become worse; in fact, it could very easily become a negative demand state. As a result, the image of HRD will suffer greatly.

A no demand state may also be a symptom of low familiarity with HRD on the part of clients within the organization. This condition often occurs because HRD practitioners believe clients are more aware of their training programs and services than they really are. The practitioners become overconfident and begin to believe that HRD programs and services enjoy a very favorable reputation among their clients when they do not. In Chapter One, we saw how a condition of low familiarity and favorability results in a bankrupted HRD program. A no demand state, then, can become an even worse condition, and HRD practitioners facing one must become proactive in an effort to prevent further erosion of their image.

Three different types of training programs and services are characterized by a no demand state. First, there are those that are perceived as having little or no value to the organization. As discussed previously, training programs and services that provide little or no value cannot be exchanged by clients. Each program must be examined to determine how it can be improved to meet client demand. Appropriate changes must be incorporated and an offering reinstated.

Second, there are training programs and services that are perceived to have value but not in this particular organization. For example, a sales training program for employees who can use their skills daily is considered very valuable but not necessarily in educational institutions, government agencies, or hospitals. The utility of a training program or service is derived from the application of new knowledge, and from the provision of skills that improve employee performance and attitudes. Value is enhanced even more if the organization's effectiveness improves as a result of improved employee performance. HRD practitioners must remember that many training programs are very well designed and developed but have little or no value unless they actually relate to the situation and the needs of clients.

Third, many training programs and services fail to be demanded because clients lack knowledge of their purpose or application. Let us consider career development programs. Many employees do not understand their value or their constituent activities and so hardly use them. It is not surprising, then, that employees fail to gain an appreciation of such programs and are prevented from receiving their benefits.

The process of altering no demand is known as *stimulational marketing* (Kotler, 1987). This demand state is as difficult to alter as is negative demand because the clients do not recognize a need for the training program or service being offered by the HRD program. However, HRD practitioners can proceed in one of three ways. First, they should try to connect training programs or services to an existing performance problem in the organization. For example, an educational institution with a negative image could use a quality service training program. The HRD practitioners could design, develop, and implement such a program for the institution's administrators. The program's expressed purpose would be to develop the skills required to enhance the quality of services offered to clients. The long-term effect of the skills developed through the training program would be an improved image of the institution.

Second, the HRD practitioners must improve how clients within the organization perceive them. One approach might include becoming involved in organizational development activities, which are designed to foster change in the organization. This will help clients view HRD as a developmental process rather than an overhead expense to the organization.

The third approach that HRD practitioners could use is a comprehensive promotional strategy designed to communicate the intent, purpose, advantages, benefits, and values of HRD. It would include altering the organization's receptiveness to training programs and services. One way of accomplishing this would be to distribute information on the value of HRD to essential centers of influence as well as important members of the client group (see Chapter Nine for more information).

Latent Demand and Developmental Marketing. A condition where clients share a common learning deficiency, performance problem, or developmental need but where relevant training programs or services do not exist is known as *latent demand.* Consider the following example. Several supervisors within an organization feel inadequate when they conduct employee performance appraisals. In addition, they have not communicated this developmental need to their superiors. As a result, it has not been communicated to HRD practitioners either, and a training program has not been developed to address it. Thus the supervisors continue to perform employee performance appraisals without proper training. If the need were known, an appropriate training program could be designed, developed, and implemented. This demand state provides HRD practitioners with a unique opportunity to improve their value to the organization. Their primary effort should be to identify existing needs and create training programs and services that address them. This process is known as *developmental marketing* (Kotler, 1987).

Traditional needs assessment methods are best here. They include questionnaires, interviews, group discussions, nominal group technique (consensus decision-making group) reports and records, observation, and work samples. Each is designed to identify existing learning and development needs, and each has its advantages and disadvantages. It is therefore best to use a combination of methods to secure optimal results (Gilley and Eggland, 1989).

Faltering Demand and Remarketing. All training programs and services, regardless of their importance and popularity, experience a period of diminishing demand. This situation could be caused by an obsolescence of the knowledge or skills developed. The condition, in which further decline is expected, is known as *faltering demand* (Kotler, 1987).

In many cases the decline is very gradual and is often not noticed by HRD practitioners until it becomes serious. Some training programs and services, in contrast, become popular very quickly but decline in popularity at an equally rapid rate. These are known as fads. (We discuss in detail the growth and decline of training programs and services in Chapter Six when we examine the "concept life cycle.") The principal responsibilities for HRD practitioners in this situation is to discover new ways for clients to utilize the training programs and services. The formal term for this approach is *remarketing* (Kotler, 1987).

Remarketing may require a complete redesign of the training programs as well as a change in its name or title. Services may have to be expanded or combined to enhance interest. A search for new clients within the organization is also in order. It is inappropriate to conduct an extensive promotional program for training programs and services experiencing faltering demand unless they are redesigned, renamed, and/or improved. Most HRD clients, after all, are familiar with them already but have elected to no longer utilize them. Remember, the problem in this situation is a loss of interest because training programs and services are no longer addressing the performance problems and developmental needs of clients.

Full Demand and Maintenance Marketing. This condition is an HRD practitioner's dream come true. It exists when the present level of demand equals the HRD practitioner's ability to meet it. If this condition exists, the image of HRD is enhanced. However, it is not a time for HRD practitioners to relax and become passive. Demand can change rapidly because the needs of employees change daily for such reasons as increased competition, management changes, reorganizations, mergers, and changing technology.

HRD practitioners must anticipate the decisions of management and prepare accordingly. They must also account for external forces such as an economic downturn or governmental intervention that can impact full demand. They must develop plans for expansion and growth in anticipation of ever-increasing demand plans that include additional staff, expanded facilities, new training programs and services. HRD practitioners must also become aware of internal political constraints, management shifts, and economic budget reductions, for each of these can impact the delivery of training programs and services. They must be able to identify signs of faltering demand and must examine the organizational, cultural, and technological changes that will reduce or accelerate it. Finally, they must constantly be examining the organization to determine areas of need that can be addressed.

The process of maintaining a constant awareness of market conditions is known as *maintenance marketing* (Kotler, 1987). Its primary purpose is to identify external and internal forces that threaten to erode and/or accelerate demand. Maintenance marketing also requires HRD practitioners to develop corrective measures to address ever-changing conditions.

Overfull Demand and Demarketing. On occasion, the demand for training programs and services exceeds HRD practitioners' ability to adequately deliver them. Because of this, any attempt to meet excessive demand under such circumstances may result in inferior training programs and services, greatly reducing the effectiveness and possibly hurting the image of HRD within the organization. This condition is often referred to as "growing too fast" and in marketing is known as overfull demand. HRD practitioners have only one realistic reaction here: to reduce demand until it is no longer excessive. They need to encourage certain if not all client groups to reduce their usage of HRD, whether temporarily or permanently. In other words, they need to use marketing in reverse. This is referred to as *demarketing*.

The situation presents HRD practitioners with a very difficult problem. HRD programs, as we have said, are established to provide employees with knowledge and skills that enable the organization to be more productive and profitable. In short, HRD's function is to serve the organization. Its failure to do so could be considered indifferent or lack of competence and greatly impact its future effectiveness. One approach that could prevent a negative reaction is to have a frank and open conversation with upper management or decision makers explaining the situation, the circumstances, and the outcomes that may result unless additional resources are allocated. This will be received more openly than excuses for failure. The key component in this type of situation is communication (see Chapter Eight for more information).

Reviewing the Demand States and Marketing Responses. Each of the demand states previously discussed presents HRD practitioners with a different dilemma (Figure 2.5). Each must be analyzed in order that the correct marketing response can be used. It should be noted that more than one state can occur simultaneously, because a demand state is directly affected by each segment of the client group. In other words, executives can have perceptions of HRD and its training programs and services that differ from those of managers, supervisors, and employees. These different perceptions will produce different demand states within the same organization, resulting in multiple demand states that HRD practitioners must take into account.

The best marketing response is to develop a strategic marketing plan for the HRD program. In this way, all demand states will be identified and the most appropriate marketing strategies can then be used. The image of HRD and its practitioners will be the benefactors of this approach.

Figure 2.5. HRD Demand States and Marketing Responses.

Demand States	Marketing Task	Formal Name
1. Negative Demand	Reverse Demand	Conversional
2. No Demand	Create Demand	Stimulational
3. Latent Demand	Develop Demand	Developmental
4. Faltering Demand	Revitalize Demand	Remarketing
5. Full Demand	Maintain Demand	Maintenance
6. Overfull Demand	Reduce Demand	Demarketing

Source: Adapted from Kotler, 1987, p. 23. Adapted by permission of Prentice-Hall, Inc., Englewood Cliffs, N.J. 07632.

Conclusion

We have stated elsewhere (Gilley and Eggland, 1989) that HRD practitioners must learn to understand, plan, and manage exchanges. This means HRD practitioners must develop skills in researching and understanding clients' performance problems and developmental needs. Simultaneously, practitioners must design training programs that meet those problems and needs. They must also effectively communicate the advantages, benefits, and values of training programs and services to potential clients.

In summary, marketing of HRD programs is simple. It requires HRD practitioners to design, develop, and implement training programs and provide services that bring about voluntary exchanges of value with clients. These exchanges should produce knowledge and skills that help the organization to achieve its operational results. For this reason, HRD practitioners should incorporate the marketing concept into every training program and service offered.

HRD practitioners must also become knowledgeable about the concept of demand and the various demand states facing HRD programs. Based on this understanding, informative decisions can be made and appropriate marketing strategies can be identified and applied.

Chapter Three

Generating Interest and Participation in Training

When executives, managers, supervisors, and employees choose to participate in training programs or HRD services, they engage in a series of activities known as the *adoption process*. HRD practitioners must understand the complexities of this process in order to be of service to their clients and, as a result, develop promotional activities that communicate the values of HRD to management. The adoption process can also be used to determine the types of training programs and services that will improve performance and satisfy developmental needs. In addition, the factors affecting the adoption process will also affect the selection of training programs and HRD services. Each of these components will be examined in this chapter.

The adoption process is essentially one of making decisions. HRD clients are faced with making decisions every day. Sometimes these decisions are simple and routine and require little effort; at other times they are difficult and complex and require a great deal of time and effort. Therefore, it is important that HRD practitioners understand the essential phases of the decision-making process. We believe a common five-step process can be seen at work regardless of the type of decision being made.

Learning about the adoption process provides insight into how HRD clients choose to participate in training programs and/ or to use HRD services. In order to better understand the process, we will examine the following:

- Stages of the adoption process
- Individual differences in the selection of training programs and services
- The role of personal influence in selection

By examining these three areas, you will better understand why clients select certain training programs and services over others. You will also be better able to incorporate changes in training programs and services in order to accommodate client needs. Familiarity with the adoption process will help you improve your timing of new programs and services as well as refine your evaluation strategies and restructure your promotional activities.

Stages of the Adoption Process

HRD clients go through a series of stages when they consider adopting a training program or HRD service. According to Rogers ([1962] 1983), these stages are

1. *Becoming aware of performance problems and developmental needs.* HRD clients become aware of problems and needs affecting their performance and effectiveness.
2. *Developing interest.* HRD clients seek information about alternatives designed to meet their needs and solve their problems. This includes developing interest in appropriate training programs or services.
3. *Evaluating alternatives.* HRD clients consider the advantages and benefits of training programs and services and determine whether or not to participate in or use them.
4. *Selecting an alternative.* HRD clients establish criteria for selecting an alternative and then apply them to training programs and services.
5. *Adopting an alternative and evaluating the selection.* HRD clients decide to participate in a training program or utilize an HRD service. They then independently evaluate their selection and determine if it meets their needs or has solved their problem.

Each of these will be examined in detail in this chapter.

Stage 1: Becoming Aware of Needs

In order to fully understand the adoption process it is essential to identify how performance problems and development needs arise. A problem exists when there is a difference between what people have and what they want. This may also be referred to as a need. Thus awareness begins with the identification of performance problems and developmental needs. To illustrate consider the following situation. The consultants of a large human resource management consulting firm maintain moderate selling skills. This condition is known as the "what is" state. They desire to develop advanced selling skills in order to be more effective in client presentations. The desired state is known as the "what should be" condition. A problem or need exists when this "gap" between the current state and desired state affects or impacts the productivity and efficiency of the consultants. Therefore, the adoption process begins with the identification of problems or needs that require some type of action on the part of employees.

People choose to participate in training programs for a variety of reasons. One of the most common is that they have identified a knowledge or skill deficiency that affects their performance and/or career options. Organizations are also motivated to address these performance deficiencies because it will greatly improve their efficiency and profitability to do so. If both the employees and the organization begin to address the problems and needs, the result could be a cycle that provides momentum for HRD programs.

It is important to remember that performance problems and needs differ in their degree of seriousness or urgency. Some require immediate action while others require little more than identification. Because of time constraints and limited resources, HRD practitioners can only react to a select number of their clients' requests. Therefore, they must prioritize them.

One way is to consider the importance of each request in relation to its urgency. Figure 3.1 illustrates how this can be done. Each request must first be evaluated regarding its importance. HRD practitioners must then decide if the request must be addressed immediately or can be delayed. Clients' requests that are both highly

Figure 3.1. Prioritizing Clients' Requests.

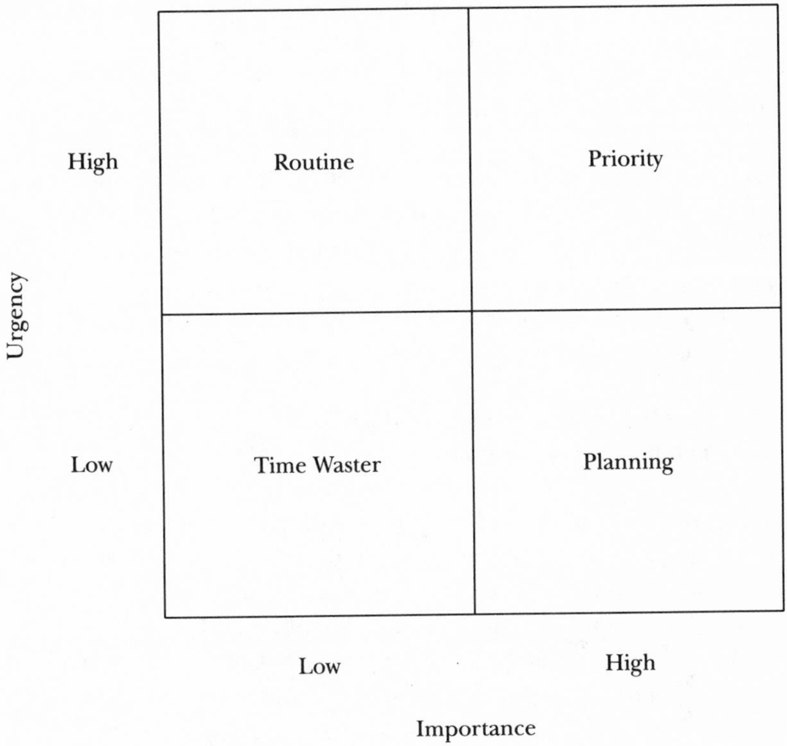

	Low Importance	High Importance
High Urgency	Routine	Priority
Low Urgency	Time Waster	Planning

important and highly urgent are considered "priorities." They must be addressed immediately. Requests that are less important but still urgent are considered "routine." Such requests must be a part of the HRD practitioner's everyday offerings of training programs and services but the financial and human resources needed to support them should be limited. Requests that are highly important but not urgent are referred to as "planning." They are considered important because they have future productivity or performance implications. Therefore, these requests should be part of the HRD program's long-term offerings. Meeting these problems or needs could greatly enhance the credibility and image of HRD. Finally, requests that are classified as low in importance and urgency are considered "time wasters" and HRD practitioners would be wise to avoid spending time and resources on them.

Once the requests have been ranked, HRD practitioners will have to determine the amount of time to spend on each one.

Stage 2: Developing Interest

Once HRD clients have identified their performance problems and developmental needs and HRD practitioners have ranked them by importance and urgency, the clients enter into the information gathering phase of the adoption process. During this phase, HRD clients begin to develop interest in the interventions designed to help them.

How do HRD clients gather information and deal with decision situations?

We have identified two types of information gatherers who are common during this phase. The first type are known as *determined information searchers*. They are very active and involved in their search for information; indeed, they are often viewed as being on a mission during a search. They will utilize several sources of information such as catalogs, professional journals, interviews with former users, attendance at professional conferences, direct inquiries, and personal networks. Randy Tomassi, senior member of the Central Region Human Resources Development Committee of William M. Mercer, identifies these information searchers as being "very in touch with their career objectives and goals."

The second type are less active and involved in their search for information. We refer to them as *passive information searchers*. They are more casual and informal, seldom using more than two sources from which to gather information. Passive information searchers prefer to rely on the opinions of other people regarding the effectiveness and value of the training programs and/or HRD services that they are considering.

We have also found that the amount and type of information gathering increases as clients move to more complex and important decisions. We have identified three types of decision situations among HRD clients. Just as each requires a different level of information gathering, so do the responsibilities of HRD practitioners vary with each.

We call the first *routine decision making*. It is the simplistic type of decision situation and is characterized by low involvement and commitment. The decision is made quickly with little mental effort. The decision to attend a luncheon seminar that requires little involvement would be an example of this type of decision situation. Participants are not required to change behavior or correct performance problems as a result of this type of program. They can be passive observers, gathering information that is not designed to challenge their current knowledge or levels of performance.

HRD practitioners in this type of situation have two responsibilities. First, they must continuously reinforce the value of their seminars by emphasizing their quality and usefulness. Second, they must demonstrate that the time spent in the seminar is more important than having lunch alone or with one's colleagues. Both responsibilities call for using the exchange process as a model.

The second type of decision situation is referred to as *limited problem solving*. It is more complex than routinized decision making because HRD clients are confronted with the selection of unknown variables that they must consider. These include the material and information addressed during training, the training methods used, the activities required of participants during training, the behavior changes required as a result of participating and the follow-up exercises or activities required in order to reinforce learning and/or behavior changes. Each of these must be addressed by HRD clients before making a decision.

When clients are facing this type of decision situation, you must recognize that they are trying to reduce risk through information gathering. Therefore, you should design a communication program that will explain your training programs and services. Special attention should be given to the variables just outlined. Information on the advantages and benefits of each training program and service should also be provided, in order to describe how training programs and services differ and why some are better than others.

The third type of decision situation is referred to as *extensive problem solving*. Decision making reaches its greatest complexity when clients face unfamiliar training programs and services and have not established criteria to evaluate them. In this situation, considerable time and effort is spent seeking out alternatives, searching for information about them, and evaluating the information. This is done in an attempt to determine which one will be most effective.

Many of our clients face this decision situation when trying to decide between using internal or external HRD practitioners. For example, the selection of an organizational development (OD) consultant, hired to help create a service-oriented culture for an organization, falls in this category. The problem facing HRD clients is that they are unfamiliar with the activities required to produce the desired outcomes. In addition, most of them have no criteria for evaluating and selecting an OD consultant. Therefore, many hours must be spent by them identifying the qualities to look for in a consultant or consulting firm, the type of services provided, the approach used, the expectations of and commitment required from organizational members, and the outcomes to be realized on completion of the project. The internal and external HRD practitioners must then be measured against these criteria in order to identify acceptable candidates.

As an internal HRD practitioner, your task is to help your clients better understand the requirements of this type of HRD intervention, as well as its value and importance. This will help the clients establish measurable outcomes with more confidence. A second responsibility is that you must communicate your professional experience as well as provide examples of your work. This will demonstrate the quality of the services you offer. Such actions often require face-to-face contact with clients to describe your skills and abilities. Simply stated, you are responsible for educating your clients about the services you can provide and how you can best deliver them to the organization. In this way, you will be better able to compete with the external HRD practitioners who also desire to provide services to your organization.

What are the primary information sources that HRD clients use when making decisions?

HRD clients rely on a number of information sources when gathering data used in decision situations. We have identified six: colleagues, organizational networks (including mentors), professional networks, supervisors and managers, the organizational traditions and culture, and promotional material provided by HRD practitioners.

Most HRD clients are often exposed to all of these information sources. Each has advantages and disadvantages. A critical question that must be answered by HRD practitioners is which source or combinations of sources do HRD clients rely on when making their decisions. The answer to this question will provide valuable insight into the adoption process. It will also help HRD practitioners develop strategies to influence as well as improve the quality of the clients' information source.

Let us look at this process through the eyes of a new college graduate who joined a large professional service firm six months ago. The employee is interested in developing supervisory management skills. She has been identified as an "up-and-coming star," and for that reason the organization is interested in providing a fast track of development for her.

Her search for information begins with informal discussions with a number of her colleagues. Each person provides personal perceptions of the development approaches available. Most of the information is based upon that person's experience and knowledge of career planning and development. The information gathered here, while informative, is not very reliable. In fact, it is often the most inaccurate information source, which is one of the problems with relying on it too much. Unfortunately, too many HRD clients are guilty of just that.

If the employee has developed a mentor relationship, she can also seek this person's advice. This is a very important resource because of the influence the mentor can have on an employee. If the mentor possesses the background and experience to provide quality advice, the relationship can be an invaluable source of information. Such relationships, however, are often informal and voluntary. This can present several problems. The employee may take the relationship much more seriously than the mentor; she may even believe a mentoring relationship exists when one does not. The result may be less than frank and honest information sharing. Mentors may also provide information that is outdated; much of their experience, after all, is several years old. Thus past solutions may not provide answers to present problems.

The employee we are dealing with has not been in the work force long enough to establish a strong professional network. If one has been developed, it most likely is made up of younger, less experienced professionals. Therefore, the information shared will be limited. If the employee were several years older, this source of information could prove to be important to her. The one drawback to using this source is that the differences in circumstances from one organization to another can influence the information being shared. This can seriously bias the information being presented. It must be filtered to protect the employee from incorrect advice.

Supervisors and managers can be the very best source of information for this type of employee. In fact it is their responsibility to provide her with the information she needs. Two problems exist, however. First, the supervisor or manager may be uninformed about the situation or lack the skills needed to provide information and advice in a clear and concise manner. Second, the relationship between this employee and her supervisor or manager may not be very strong; in fact, the latter may resent the growth opportunities made available to her and give her inaccurate information to prevent her from reaching her potential. At the same time, the employee may not trust her immediate supervisor's or manager's advice, seeing it as unreliable and unqualified.

Nevertheless, many organizations see this source of information as their most valuable one. They have created training programs designed to improve the career planning and development skills of supervisors and managers. They believe that supervisors and managers must also develop performance appraisal skills designed to "feed" the career planning and development process. One such organization is LTV. Chuck Butters, LTV's director of human resources development, has stated that "supervisors are the companies' frontline partner in the improvement of performance and quality. This can only be done if they provide sound career planning advice for their employees. In addition, our performance appraisal program can provide needed development information for all our employees. . . . The performance appraisals program is the backbone for growth and development of our employees" (personal conversation with Gilley, September 1990).

Organizational traditions and culture can also be an excellent source of information for our employee, providing her with a historical context to follow. This is true even for fast-track employees. In fact, avoiding organizational traditions and culture can limit an employee's understanding of operational procedures and decision making and deprive her of a sense of how things get done in that organization. Bypassing organizational traditions can cause resentment in other employees who may then place roadblocks in the way of future opportunities.

Commonality among employees is another form of awareness that organizational traditions foster. Let us illustrate our point. Bud Baskin, director of quality and organizational development at Arthur Andersen, says that "all of their twenty thousand employees share a common experience. Every employee, international or national, participates in training programs at our facility in St. Charles, Illinois. This provides a shared experience with each and every employee. In this way, we believe our employees view the company as a more personal organization" (personal conversation with Gilley, March 1989). This type of strong organizational tradition is something that employees have to reckon with.

The final information source—promotional material provided by HRD practitioners—can include catalogs of training programs and HRD services provided by the HRD program. As previously discussed, they should outline the material and information provided, the training methods used, the participant activities, the performance changes required, and the follow-up procedures used to enhance learning transfer. The advantages and benefits received should be identified in order to clearly communicate the outcomes of each training program and service. Catalogs should provide the time, date, and location of the training program. The employee can use this type of information source to identify the types of programs available and so obtain the knowledge and skills desired.

Stage 3: Evaluating Alternatives

Once HRD clients have gathered information about training programs and services that they believe will improve performance problems and satisfy developmental needs, they must assess them and identify alternatives. We have identified five steps required to accomplish this task (Figure 3.2).

The process can best be illustrated by an actual example. At the beginning of each year, the central region HRD Committee of William M. Mercer introduces their human resource development programs to their consultants, who are required to select two courses to participate in during the year. Therefore, the process begins with the distribution of the central region HRD catalog. All possible training programs are identified. The catalog includes the name of each program, its outline and objectives, its advantages and benefits, the training methods and activities involved, and its time, date, and location. The listing of all possibilities is known as the *total set;* it includes ten training programs. The total set can be divided into two categories: the *awareness set,* consisting of the programs with which the consultants are familiar; and the *unawareness set,* consisting of those with which they are not familiar. The awareness set can be a very small list if the consultants are not familiar with the training programs offered by the HRD program.

The information gathering phase begins at this point. Each of the six sources of information reviewed in the previous section is used to develop a better understanding of each training program. At this point all training programs are still being considered. Of the training programs in which the consultants are interested, however, they will only seriously consider a limited number. This list represents the consultants' *consideration set.* The other training programs are relegated to an *infeasible set.* After additional information has been gathered about the training programs in the consideration set, a few remain of greater interest. These constitute the *choice set;* the remainder are placed in the *nonchoice set.* The final phase is a careful evaluation of the choice set followed by final selection referred to as the *decision* (Kotler, 1987).

What evaluation models do HRD clients use when selecting training programs and services?

HRD practitioners must understand that each training program and service offered consists of different attributes that are used by

Figure 3.2. Evaluating Programs and Services: The Process of Evaluation.

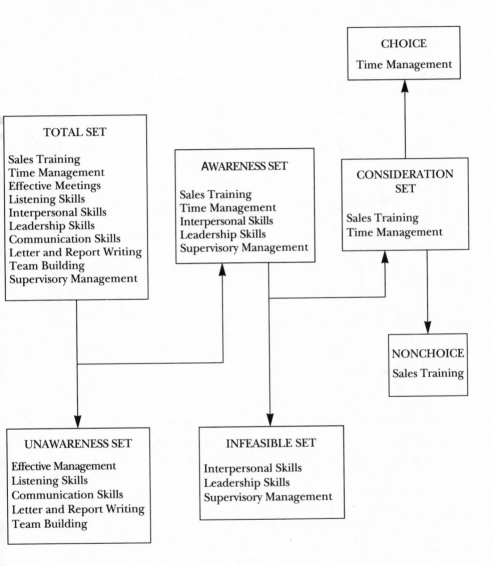

Source: William M. Mercer, Inc. Reprinted by permission.

clients to make a selection. An attribute is defined as a characteristic or component of a training program or service that separates it from others. Attributes could include the type of information or skills to be developed; the time, date, and location of the training program; the type of exercises and activities used during the program; the training methods used; and type of follow-up activities required. Attributes can be prioritized by HRD clients in one of three ways:

1. Each attribute can be assigned a different value or weight. Training programs or services that do not reach the highest rank are no longer considered, while the ones that have the highest total rank are selected. This is the simplest way of prioritizing training programs and services; it is known as the *ranking method*. HRD clients can use this method to establish the consideration set and also as a way of deciding what training programs and services should be identified as part of the choice set. Lastly, the ranking method can be used to make their final selection.

2. Each attribute can be rated as to its importance by using a predetermined scale. Here HRD clients will rank the attributes (e.g., location, time, method of instruction) in order of importance. In this method, all training programs in the choice set are compared to the highest-ranked attribute and the one that most closely matches the attribute is selected. If more than one meets the highest-ranked attribute, the next highest is used to separate programs and this process continues until a program is selected. For example, Cindy Diddion, director of training with ISCO Environmental Division in Lincoln, Nebraska, has used this model in the selection of a supervisory training program. The attribute considered most important was "the use of both positive and negative examples of supervision." This was considered very important to the transferability of knowledge and skill for their employees. Several programs were reviewed and only one training program met this criterion. As a result, it was selected and used. This is known as the *rating method*.

3. The total value of all attributes is identified. A 100-point scale is the most common reference used. To make a selection, this method considers all the attributes of a training program or service rather than just a single attribute. The programs or services in the consideration set are compared by evaluating each of the attributes

identified. The program having the highest overall score would become the selection of the HRD clients. This method is very useful when the weakness of one attribute is compensated by the strengths of others. It is known as the *sum total method*.

These methods are often used by clients in an informal manner; many times, indeed, they are unaware that they are using any of them. Nevertheless, the methods are common practice and can be identified through interviews with clients. The primary implication for HRD practitioners is that training programs and services consist of attributes that clients review in order to make a selection.

How can HRD practitioners modify or alter their training programs and services in response to the evaluation models?

HRD practitioners can gain insight into how HRD clients select training programs and services by interviewing a representative sample of participants. Such an analysis can produce a number of suggestions for improvement. As a result, HRD practitioners can develop strategies to improve their training programs and services as well as their HRD. We have identified the following:

1. Modify the training programs or services to better meet the developmental needs and performance problems of clients.
2. Alter clients' perception of the training program and services through promotional materials and face-to-face discussions, which may also include the organizational leaders, managers, and supervisors who serve as opinion leaders and mentors within the organization.
3. Alter the attributes of training programs and services in order to meet HRD clients' expectations.
4. Modify decision makers' perception of the "ideal" training programs and services. It is important for participants to recognize what they will receive as a result of participating in a program or service. Realistic expectations will benefit HRD practitioners and help enhance the image of HRD.

Stage 4: Selecting an Alternative

To many, the selection of training programs and services is merely the process of evaluating alternatives. However, at least four kinds of factors can interfere with this process: the attitudes of others, the degree of perceived risk, social factors, and psychological factors. These combine to make up a *selection filter* that is used by HRD clients (Figure 3.3).

Attitudes of Others. If a training program or service is not supported by others in the organization, the probability of its adoption will be greatly reduced. Further, negative attitudes toward HRD in general can be very intense, and this too may impact the ultimate selection decision. The critical question that HRD clients must answer is, Will they comply with the external pressure exerted by others in the organization? For example, if negative criticism is coming from a colleague within the organization, it may be less important than if it were being shared by an executive—a situation that could affect their career opportunities. If HRD clients elect to participate in training programs that are negatively perceived, they will have to justify their decision to others.

Perceived Risk. After evaluating several alternatives and selecting a training program or service, HRD clients must still consider the amount of risk they are willing to take. There are both social and psychological risks in making a final selection, and HRD clients will ultimately be held accountable for it. This may be the reason many of them delay selecting training programs and services.

Social Factors. The next layer of the selection filter consists of social factors. These factors have a great influence on HRD clients. They include reference groups and centers of influence. A *reference group* refers to the collection of people who influence HRD clients' attitudes, beliefs, opinions, and values regarding selection. It can be further subdivided into primary and secondary groups. A *primary group* such as a close friend, colleague, or fellow worker maintains direct influence and constant contact with HRD clients. *Secondary groups*, on the other hand, have less direct influence on or contact

Figure 3.3. Factors That Filter the Selection of Programs and Services.

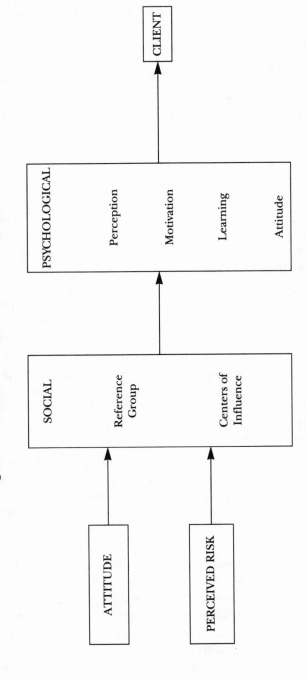

with an HRD client but do, however, serve as a reflection of opinion. An example of this type of person would be a member of a professional society, with whom the relationship is very casual and the frequency of contact approximately once a year.

Reference groups can significantly influence HRD clients in three ways:

- They can expose them to possible developmental needs and areas of performance deficiency.
- They can identify the type of training programs and/or services available to address performance problems and developmental needs.
- They can alter the HRD client's perception of training programs and/or services.

Another social group that may influence HRD clients consists of *centers of influence,* also referred to as *mentors* or *opinion leaders.* They manifest themselves in dyadic relationships. Centers of influence maintain very strong relationships with HRD clients. One of the reasons for this is that they exhibit outstanding leadership qualities, charisma, credibility, and persuasive skills. Because of these personal traits, they can greatly influence the opinions of HRD clients regarding the selection of training programs or services. Centers of influence, however, may not be subject matter or career development experts, and this could reduce the quality of their advice. The failure of most HRD clients to recognize these shortcomings of theirs can be a very serious blind spot. Reference groups and centers of influence are social factors. They combine to make up the third layer of the selection filter.

Psychological Factors. The most influential factors affecting HRD clients during the selection process are the psychological ones, more specifically perceptions, motives, learning, and attitudes. These "internal" personal factors are of the greatest influence because they are the most interpersonal in nature. Indeed, they combine to make up the principal elements of human behavior.

People often have different perceptions of the same situation. This is because information is acquired through one or more of the five senses: sight, hearing, smell, touch, and taste. Conclusions are drawn based upon the quality and quantity of information gathered. However, the sensory information is attended, organized, and interpreted in different manners. This process is known as *perception*.

To better understand how perceptions affect selection it will be necessary to examine how information is identified, organized, and interpreted. The process begins with the acquisition of information inputs known as *stimuli* (Ferrell and Pride, 1982). Each day, HRD clients are exposed to a tremendous number of stimuli. Because they are too numerous to take in at one time, the majority of them will be ignored. We refer to this process as *selective attention*. Of the stimuli that pass through one's perceptual filter, each is subject to personal interpretation and analysis. This is because HRD clients, like many other people, maintain different awarenesses, understandings, beliefs, attitudes, and values. As a result, they alter the incoming stimuli to "fit" their perceptions. This process of twisting or shaping information into personal meaning is known as *selective distortion*. The third process causes HRD clients to have different perceptions of the same stimuli. This is a process that enables them to retain information that supports their attitudes, beliefs, and values while rejecting information that is contrary or irrelevant. It is known as *selective retention*. The presence of these three perceptual mechanisms (selective attention, distortion, and retention) means that HRD practitioners must develop promotional activities and adopt marketing strategies that break through the very strong perceptual filters of HRD clients.

The second psychological factor that affects HRD clients concerns the *motives* they have about training, motives that could affect their willingness to participate in training programs as well as utilize HRD services. This factor will ultimately affect their selection of training programs and services. As a result, HRD practitioners must identify such motives and react accordingly in order to ensure adoption.

The third psychological factor is known as *learning*. When HRD clients participate in training programs or use HRD services, they experience direct and indirect effects that influence their future behavior. For many of them, selecting a training program is no more than random participation in the hope that the most appropriate and effective one was selected. This hit-or-miss approach fails to adequately address their developmental needs and performance deficiencies.

However, HRD is often blamed when positive and productive change does not occur. Therefore, the hit-and-miss approach must be eliminated and replaced with a more systematic and strategic approach. Once positive change occurs, the attitudes of HRD clients toward training will improve, starting a cycle of participation that will lead to further growth and development. Such positive experiences will enhance future selection on the part of HRD clients.

Therefore, participation in training programs or using HRD services produces learning affects the *attitudes* of HRD clients. This is the fourth psychological factor in selection. Attitudes are deeply rooted and interact with many other attitudes; thus they are very hard to modify. To do so, in fact, may require painful adjustment in many other attitudes. An HRD client's attitude toward training may therefore be very difficult to alter and may require HRD practitioners to develop very extensive and expensive promotional activities. This approach will be further addressed in Chapters Eight and Nine.

Each of the layers of the selection filter can either crystallize HRD clients' selection or severely distort it. Perhaps it would be more accurate to say that each layer will positively or negatively affect the training program or HRD service selected. Thus these factors must be taken into consideration by HRD practitioners before they design, develop, or implement training programs or offer services. They should also be considered before the creation of promotional programs and activities. Finally, HRD practitioners must understand the complexity of the selection process and account for the many factors influencing HRD clients, for without this understanding they may continue to place unrealistic demands and pressures on them. In addition, HRD programs will continue to offer training programs and services that are not perceived as improving performance problems or satisfying developmental needs. This will continue to produce a negative image of HRD.

Stage 5: Evaluating the Selection

According to Engel and Blackwell (1982), researchers have discovered two common reactions among people who have just made a decision.

We feel both are applicable to HRD situations. They are known as *postdecision dissonance* and *satisfaction and/or dissatisfaction.*

Postdecision Dissonance. HRD clients who have second thoughts after their decision often suffer from a condition known as postdecision dissonance. It is brought about by tension created by uncertainty about the decision's "correctness" (McCarthy and Perreault, 1984). Many even wonder if another alternative would have been a better choice. This condition can bring about distortions in the satisfaction levels HRD clients experience related to their choices (Barry, 1986). In addition, many HRD clients feel abandoned by HRD practitioners after participating in training programs or using HRD services. This, too, can lead to postdecision dissonance.

Satisfaction or Dissatisfaction. Most HRD clients will experience some level of satisfaction or dissatisfaction after participating in a training program or using an HRD service. Swan and Combs (1976) refer to satisfaction/dissatisfaction as the *expectations-performance theory.* They maintain that the clients' level of satisfaction is directly related to their expectation of how the training program or HRD service will perform. If the expectations are met, the clients will be highly satisfied. If, however, the training program or service fails to meet their expectations, they will be dissatisfied or even openly critical of it.

Implications for HRD Practitioners. In order to prevent postdecision dissonance and dissatisfaction, HRD practitioners should not make claims about their training programs and services that cannot be realized. This should help match the training programs' and services' performance outcomes with clients' expectations. It might even be wise to understate performance outcomes so that the client will experience higher-than-expected satisfaction.

HRD practitioners should conduct follow-up activities and exercises whenever possible. These will reduce HRD clients' fears of being abandoned. If you cannot conduct them yourself, appoint a course leader to do so. This will accomplish three things: it will demonstrate your confidence in the participants; it will foster self-directed inquiry on the part of the participants; and it will help improve teamwork after the training program has been completed.

We also suggest that HRD practitioners should develop effective postselection communication with their clients in order to reassure them that they have made the right decision. Finally, HRD practitioners should monitor the attitudes of HRD clients in order to obtain an accurate picture of how training programs and services are being perceived. If the clients report dissatisfaction or postdecision dissonance, appropriate changes should be made.

Individual Differences in Selection

Some HRD clients are the first to participate in training programs and services while others avoid participating as long as possible. Why should such differences exist? When we examined this phenomenon, we discovered that one of the primary reasons for this behavior is a concept known as *innovativeness*. This refers to people's tolerance for uncertainty: the better they deal with uncertainty, the more venturesome they are. On the other hand, some people would prefer to wait until a training program or service has been well tested before they participate. Whatever the reason, HRD practitioners must account for both types of client and for those in the middle.

Rogers ([1962] 1983), in his classic study of how innovations are adopted, has identified five different categories of people, with the percentage of the total population that falls into each and each one's dominant value.

1. Innovators (2.5 percent). Rogers reports that the dominant value of innovators is *venturesomeness*. They like to take risks and be the first to try new training programs or HRD services. Only 2.5 percent of the population falls into this category, according to Rogers. Therefore, HRD practitioners should not expect new training programs and services to be selected by a large number of clients. The only clients that will participate are those who are willing to take a risk.

2. Early adopters (13.5 percent). The dominant value of early adopters, who make up 13.5 percent of the population, is that of *respect*. They perceive themselves as centers of influence and enjoy the role of influencing others regarding training programs or ser-

vices. They will adopt training programs and services early, but with discretion. When this group begins to participate, HRD practitioners can begin to see the momentum developing for new training programs and services. More resources are needed to accommodate this group. Thus, HRD practitioners must be able to recognize when the early adopters are participating and make adjustments accordingly.

3. Early majority (34 percent). The group known as the early majority represents one of the largest segments of the population. Its dominant value is *deliberateness*. People of this type prefer to participate in training programs and services before the majority of HRD clients do. However, they do not see themselves as leaders within the organization, although their involvement places training programs and services in great demand. In Chapter Six, we refer to this as the *growth stage*. The primary implication for HRD practitioners is that they must be prepared to meet the demand. Resources used to deliver other, less-demanded programs and services may have to be shifted and used to deliver training programs and services that involve this group.

4. Late majority (34 percent). The fourth category can be best described as skeptics; in fact, *skepticism* is their dominant value. The late majority make up another large segment of the population at 34 percent, tying the early majority. They delay making their move until most of the population have decided to participate in training programs and use HRD services. As this group begins to participate, HRD practitioners must begin to consider a strategy that will help them shift their resources to other programs and services. The principal reason for this decision is that the total (statistical) population available for a training program or service has been significantly reduced. Although this group makes up a large number of people, a strategy that takes into account the diminishing numbers of possible participants will help HRD practitioners better utilize their limited resources.

5. Laggards (16 percent). The dominant value of this group is referred to by Rogers as *ultraconservative*. Being laggards, they are suspicious of any change, innovation, new program, or service, and adopt them only because a vast majority of other people consider them acceptable. HRD clients in this category will participate

in training programs or use services when little or no risk is involved. At this point, the end is near. HRD practitioners should not invest their resources in training programs and services that are attractive to this population group. If they do, they could be viewed as dated and of little value to the organization. Such a perception is almost impossible to overcome. Resources assigned to training programs and services that are popular with this group should only meet present demand.

Role of Personal Influence

Innovators and early adopters view themselves as centers of influence. Accordingly, they spend a great deal of time influencing the thinking and actions of others, including their attitudes toward the adoption of training programs or services offered by HRD. The opinions of this group are most useful in situations where HRD clients have to place themselves at some perceived risk when selecting a training program or using an HRD service.

Another stage at which personal influence is very important is during the evaluation stage, when the ultimate value of a training program or service is decided. A positive decision will subsequently affect future decisions made by the HRD client. A negative experience, by contrast, will serve to reinforce negative attitudes toward HRD and its practitioners and will ultimately hurt the image of HRD.

Conclusion

The adoption process consists of five separate stages. They include becoming aware of performance problems and developmental needs, developing interest, evaluating alternatives, selecting an alternative, and adopting the alternative and evaluating the selection. Mostly this process will help HRD practitioners better understand why clients select certain programs and services over others. This information will help in making changes in existing programs and services and improving the designs of future ones.

We also identified several factors that impact the selection of training programs and services. These factors, attitudes, and perceived risks, social and psychological, combine to make up a *selection filter* that is used by HRD clients.

We also examined why people differ in their selection of training programs and services. We referred to this concept as innovativeness. People who are more venturesome and can deal with more uncertainty are more likely to participate in training programs and use services earlier than those who are not. We identify five separate stages of innovativeness: innovators, early adoptors, early (majority), late (majority), and laggards.

Three components of the adoption process have been outlined. Each has an impact upon the selection of training programs and the utilization of HRD services by HRD clients. HRD practitioners must understand the complexity of the adoption process and realize that the selection of training programs and services is not simple. Without this awareness, HRD practitioners will approach their clients in a very superficial and simplistic manner, and the result they desire will not occur. Finally, accounting for each of these components will help HRD practitioners design and develop better training programs and services, ones that can be critically analyzed and closely inspected by HRD clients. In addition, HRD practitioners can develop promotional programs designed to communicate the advantages and benefits of each training program and service.

Chapter Four

Initiating a Strategic Marketing Plan for HRD: The First Steps

Conventional, scientific, theoretical, and popular wisdom all converge at some point to agree on the virtues of planning for assorted endeavors. Military planning, economic planning, life planning, and social planning have all taken their turns in the limelight and are now firmly entrenched in practice.

Dimensions of Marketing

Marketing, in relative terms, has only recently secured its place in business systems as a vital force in the organization. With it have come, inevitably, the advent and subsequent refinement of the concept and practice of marketing planning. This chapter will assist the HRD professional focused on the marketing concept to answer the question, Where do I begin?

How does one begin a marketing plan?

It is said and agreed upon in virtually all quarters that little of value ever gets accomplished without a plan. Marketing is no exception to this rule. "Brochure lust" is simply not an adequate way of actualizing the marketing concept in an organization. For marketing, like any other worthy endeavor, must be done according to a plan. This plan must begin with some statement of intentions or expectations and conclude with a description of actions that are, in turn, accountable to the intentions. These concepts all have more precise meanings and descriptions that will be given life in this and subsequent chapters.

Figure 1.1 has already provided a skeletal glimpse of how the process of strategic marketing planning is configured. Predictably the model is driven by a mission. In general this is a statement reflecting the general purpose of the HRD function within the organization.

Flanking the main developmental line of the model are the situational analysis functions. The understanding here is that no useful marketing planning can occur in an environmental vacuum. The HRD market planner must look within and to the outside of the organization for input into the planning process. Profitable planning must take account of what is going on around the situation and be cognizant of the forces that are affecting it. Blithely planning for outcomes with no regard for the attendant forces likely to influence that planning is folly.

The next mainline activity in the creation of the marketing plan is the development of more specific objectives and goals for the HRD enterprise. These are normally quite amenable to measurement, grow from the mission, and are influenced by the environment or organizational culture. They might anticipate, to a modest degree, the next three activities in the model.

The foregoing activities will be delineated with care in this chapter. Subsequent chapters will deal with aspects of targeting a segmented market and with the delicate, artful, scientific combination of ingredients selected for the marketing mix. Later, suggestions will be made regarding how to form this into a strategy that will result in a dynamic marketing plan.

Why is a marketing mission statement important?

Literally every company has a mission. Often the mission is repeated at the beginning of the annual report, during speeches by executives, and in interoffice communications. It is stated in their brochures, it is conveyed to stockholders, and it is evident in the workplace. From the organization mission statement to the marketing mission statement is normally only a minor leap. It is as important to have a specific marketing mission statement as it is to have an organizational one. A marketing mission statement may involve the selling of more products, the changing of an ideology, or the provision of service to more clients. Whatever its content, it is the marketing mission statement in the HRD organization that controls and drives the marketing activity within HRD. It is this statement to which the planning model owes its origin and to which the department should profess loyalty.

It is imperative that an HRD organization have a marketing mission statement. Among other things, this gives personnel, whether internal or external to the HRD organization, a stepping-off point in establishing accountability over the program. Beyond that it becomes the identifying factor associated with activities that take place within the organization and with the arrangement of those activities into a hierarchy of importance.

The creation of a strategic marketing plan for human resource development must begin with the formulation and statement of the mission. HRD practitioners should establish a mission statement, if one does not already exist, by answering the following questions:

- What is our purpose?
- Who are our clients?
- What do we have that is valuable to our clients?
- What should our purpose be?
- What will our purpose be in the future?

This can be a very introspective and time-consuming process. Each member of the HRD organization may have a very different view of what the program is about—and what it should be about. It is, however, essential that each member of the organization finally agree and support the mission of the program. A well-developed mission statement gives everyone in the organization a sense of purpose, direction, significance, and achievement. The mission statement acts as a guide, helping to shape and form the activities of the organization members, who may be widely scattered practitioners, as they work independently and yet collectively toward the realization of the department's goals.

In the initial stages of establishing the program's scope, it will be useful for the HRD practitioner interested in marketing to work along three dimensions: the *user group*, namely, Who is to be served and satisfied; *users' needs*, namely, What is to be satisfied; and *technologies*, namely, How are users' needs to be satisfied. For example, consider an HRD program that serves only blue-collar employees who want only specialty training for their present jobs and prefer on-the-job training. This HRD organization's mission is rather narrowly defined and easily submitted to measures of accountability. Another HRD program may be much broader in scope and provide service to many clients or user groups for a variety of reasons while utilizing a large number of technological approaches. It is apparent that the missions of the two foregoing programs are not the same. Therefore, when departmental goals and objectives are established, the strategic marketing plan for each program should reflect and account for their respective differences.

To whom is a marketing mission statement responsive?

A mission statement must be responsive. In order to be so, it should answer at least two questions: responsive to whom, and to what. In this age of market segmentation and target marketing, which will be discussed in Chapter Five it is recognized that organizations—HRD organizations included—cannot be all things to all people. In general, if they try to serve everyone, they will serve no one very well. This truism leads the authors to suggest that a mission statement should be focused on needs and responsibility and that the clientele should be reasonably well-defined.

How is the marketing concept embodied in the mission statement?

Beyond this targeted definition of responsiveness, the marketing concept should be embodied in the stated marketing mission for the HRD organization. It should be quite apparent when one has read the mission statement that the organization is, without qualification, interested in satisfying the HRD needs of (a) particular client group(s). It should also be apparent that the organization is in business to satisfy clients' needs for human resource development.

The mission statement should represent a consensus. HRD mission statements should not be the product of a single individual working in a closet and emerging with a mission for the group. On the contrary, there is a McLuhanesque property that is or should be associated with the development of a marketing mission statement for HRD. That is, the process of developing the statement may be as important as the resultant statement. If we employ the philosophy that "people tend to support what they help to create," it is most important that all members of the HRD marketing enterprise have some input initially and ownership eventually in the product, that is, in the marketing mission statement.

In this regard, the HRD organization moving toward the development of a marketing mission should work to achieve a mission statement that is *feasible, motivating,* and *distinctive.* Many mission statements are not credible because they fail on these three counts. If care is not taken to make the mission statement all three, it can end up as a bland statement that is useful only on the cover of an annual report and has no chance of becoming operationalized in the workplace.

The Situational Analysis of Environments

In this day and age almost nothing occurs in a vacuum. No social, cultural, economic, geographical, or political events occur without influence from the attendant environment. This is certainly true of businesses and institutions that harbor HRD organizations. Marketing, by its very nature, requires interactions with assorted situational elements that must be accounted for in the process of marketing planning. Analyzing those environments will help the HRD department determine the opportunities and constraints that are external, as well as examine their own strengths and weaknesses, which may be internal. Another purpose of paying attention to the environments is to determine contingencies that may aid or prevent the accomplishment of the marketing mission. From this situational analysis, adjustments may be made to compensate for constraints and weaknesses while building on opportunities and strengths. There are two types of environments to be considered: internal and external.

External Environments

Internal environmental analysis considers the organization's financial condition, managerial attitudes and abilities, facilities, staffing size and quality, competitive position, image, and structure. External environmental analysis considers such elements as economic conditions, legal and political realities, social and cultural values, the state of technology, availability of resources, and competitive structure. The study of the environmental situation also helps determine events that could help or prevent the HRD department from accomplishing its marketing mission.

As we have just seen, a mission statement must exist in an environment populated with variables that will affect both the statement and its implementation. The marketing planner must work in an arena that is cognizant of this external environment. Kotler and Andreasen (1987) have suggested that the external environment affecting marketing planning can be divided into four components: the public environment, the competitive environment, the macroenvironment, and the market environment.

The *public environment* is usually thought to consist of publics that are interested in the activities of the HRD group or the parent organization. It may consist of local publics, activist publics, the general public, media publics, and regulatory agencies whose actions can affect the welfare of the organization.

The *competitive environment,* in the case of HRD departments or their parent organizations, would normally consist of groups or organizations that compete for clients, income, attention, or loyalty from the same clients that are sought by the focal organization. The competitive environment includes both current and potential competitors.

The *macroenvironment* consists of larger-scale, more generic forces that help to shape opportunities or pose threats to the organization. The main forces that must be attended to are demographic, economic, technological, political, and social. These forces are largely uncontrollable by the focal organization but they must be accommodated in the marketing plan for HRD.

Finally, the *market environment* consists of groups and organizations with whom the focal organization must cooperate in its marketing efforts. These include clients, suppliers, supporters, and marketing intermediaries. The organization must follow trends and changes in the needs, perceptions, preferences, and dissatisfactions of these key marketing cooperators.

The Public Environment. When examining the publics that affect the HRD department and its mission statement, it is necessary to acknowledge that there are several and that the strategic plan must be developed to accommodate most or all of them. A productive brainstorming session participated in by members of the HRD department will result in the identification of several publics whose interests are attendant to the department or vice versa. These publics will vary in the intensity of their association with or interest in the HRD department, but must all be acknowledged nevertheless.

There are several typologies for dividing publics into groups:

- A *welcome public* is one that likes the organization and supports the organization's goals.
- A *sought public* is one whose support the organization currently does not enjoy, but seeks somewhat aggressively.
- An *unwelcome* public is one that has some negative disposition toward the HRD department in the form of efforts to impose constraints, pressures, or controls on it.

Publics might also be classified according to the functions they perform for the organization. Here, too, there are three main groups:

1. Input publics. These are groups who supply resources to the organization. They might include, in the case of nonprofit groups, donors who make gifts of money and other assets to the organization, suppliers who sell it needed goods and services, or regulatory bodies that regulate its activities or impose certain other rules of organizational conduct.

2. Intermediary publics. These are normally enlisted as marketing intermediaries (once known as "middlemen") to help in promoting and distributing goods and services generated by the organization generally or the HRD department specifically. The HRD department, for example, might decide to offer an instructional program external to the organization and employ a program broker as a marketing intermediary to help sell it to the public.

3. Consuming publics. These consist of the various groups that consume the output of the organization or of its HRD department. They might, for instance, be clients, users, patients, subscribers, or voters.

The Competitive Environment. Any company working in the private sector and embracing an HRD department will have competitors; that is an obvious and desired fact of life in our economic system. Government and private, nonprofit organizations will also have competitors that must be recognized. Many nonprofit organizations are still inclined to deny the existence of such competition, feeling that this is characteristic only of the private sector. As a result, until recently, hospitals, schools, community agencies, museums, and so forth tended to ignore other agencies delivering similar goods and/or services. These organizations have more recently been forced to recognize that they do indeed have competitors in the form of other organizations that are striving to provide services to their clientele.

Competition should be thought of as good, not as detracting from effectiveness. The existence of two or more competitors in a marketplace vying for attention can, through advertising and other marketing efforts, stimulate increases in the size of the total market. A second value of working in a competitive environment is that it can sharpen the competitive and professional skills of the competing marketers. Sometimes, in a noncompetitive domain, deliverers of services will become complacent and the services they offer will deteriorate.

The Macroenvironment. Our world offers several broadly based forces that impact on organizations and their HRD departments generally. They can be classified as demographic, economic, technological, political-legal, and social-cultural, among other categories. Although they vary by community, state, and country, their relative impact is certain to be felt by market planners in HRD departments. Demographic and political-legal trends, for example, are very important for strategic marketing planning in social service agencies. Economic trends can be very important to charities; technological trends to organizations delivering high technology goods and services; demographic and economic trends to government agencies, as well as private sector competitors; and social-cultural trends to organizations delivering goods and services for leisure-oriented markets. These macroenvironmental factors are dynamic, not static, and have been described in several popular trend–oriented books. Newsletters and general business and social periodicals also track these macro trends in ways that can provide wisdom to the market planner for HRD.

The Market Environment. HRD managers, working to develop marketing plans, function within markets and with other entities they must work with or attempt to influence. One of these is the group of targeted consumers, which must be put at the focal point of the strategic marketing planning process. This group will be discussed in Chapter Seven. Other groups include buyers of services and goods, intermediaries used in the role of business, and other organizations, groups, or individuals positioned in the channel of distribution employed by the organization. HRD managers who are engaged in strategic marketing planning must recognize that these market players are not static entities, but are by their very nature constantly changing. In some cases, these changes are slow, methodical, and evolutionary. In other cases, they can be rapid or even chaotic. Again, keeping up with such rapid change can be facilitated by careful observation through the trade and popular press and the use of external experts.

As an aid to developing the external environment analysis for the strategic marketing plan, the HRD manager might wish to employ Exhibit 4.1. It suggests that one can define both opportunities and constraints in terms of economic conditions, the legal-political

Exhibit 4.1. Suggested Variables for Analyzing the External Environment.

External Environmental Analysis

Opportunities and Constraints

Opportunities/Constraints

1. Economic Conditions:

2. Legal-Political Environment:

3. Sociocultural Values:

4. Technological State:

5. Resource Availability:

6. Competitive Structures:

---

environment, sociocultural value, technological state, resource availability, and competitive structure.

Internal Environments

The internal environments that must be considered by the HRD manager developing a strategic marketing plan can be identified in two ways. The narrowest of those ways would be to suggest that the internal environment consists only of those people engaged directly in human resource development for the organization. A somewhat more expansive definition would include all those people employed by or associated with the organization in general. The latter is the definition to be used for purposes of this discussion. Examination of this internal environment will help the marketing planners in the HRD department determine their strengths and weaknesses. Each variable identified can affect marketing efforts. Based on this analysis, adjustments should be made to recognize and eliminate weaknesses and take advantage of the strengths that exist within the organization.

The internal environment of the organization can be identified as consisting of as many as four groups of people: the organization's board of directors, its management, its staff or employees, and any volunteers and/or consultants with close associations to it.

The HRD managers engaged in marketing efforts must first of all be responsive to those above them in the organization's hierarchy. These people would normally include the management and board of directors, but also might include legal entities, individual owners, retired influencers, and others who have a close association with the organization. There is also normally associated with most organizations an elected board of directors representing a constituent group who may be benefactors, taxpayers, owners, or in some other way interested in the fortunes of the organization. The board usually behaves in a policymaking mode, providing policies to the management of the organization. Many of those policies will have ramifications for marketing.

There is also a staff of paid employees associated with almost every organization. It includes middle management, secretaries, workers, telephone operators, and so on. This staff may also include skilled practitioners who deliver services to consumers. The staff has several competencies, skills, and limitations that must be considered when developing a marketing plan. Part of the planning process might involve motivating this staff, which would also require careful planning. In order to get the most from the staff, management must recognize that the staff wants several things from the organization including adequate salaries, fair treatment, respect and recognition, and the feeling of working for a worthwhile enterprise.

Management must create these benefits if it expects to get solid work, high morale, and continuous support in return. Employees are a "market" to which management must creatively communicate and relate.

Volunteers in many organizations are a part of the organization's operations. They perform work that requires skill and helps the organization to run efficiently. Although they are sometimes less controllable than paid staff, they are important to the organization and must be considered part of an internal public for the purpose of developing a marketing plan. Another part of the internal environmental analysis is an examination of current training facilities. It should include a realistic study of what is available in the form of technology (hardware and software) to facilitate the delivery of HRD services. This must also be studied in light of the kinds of training programs and services offered by the HRD program.

Every HRD program has a position and an image within the organization. This image should be reviewed (perhaps with the aid of an outside, independent examiner) and adjustments made in the marketing plan to accommodate it. Certain side efforts might be made to change the image so that it is consistent both with the image of the organization generally and with the specific image that the HRD department *wants* to project.

Financial considerations that affect the condition of the HRD department must be recognized. Some HRD departments have enough money to do whatever needs to be done. Others must scrape for barely adequate finances to carry out their mission in the organization.

These characteristics all combine to create a snapshot of the internal environment, which must be recognized when you are doing marketing planning. Exhibit 4.2 provides a graphic opportunity for you to write down strengths and weaknesses of your HRD program. These are only suggestions; you should feel free to add and/or subtract variables as your individual case requires.

Marketing Objectives and Goals

Once the mission statement has been developed and the external and internal environmental influences factored into the mix, it is time to begin the development of marketing objectives and goals.

Exhibit 4.2. Suggested Variables for Analyzing the Internal Environment.

Internal Environmental Analysis	
Strengths and Weaknesses	
	Strengths/Weaknesses
1. Financial Condition of Organization:	
2. Managerial Attitudes and Abilities:	
3. Present Facilities:	
4. Personnel Quality and Quantity:	
5. HRD's Competitive Position:	
6. HRD's Organizational Image:	
7. Centralized vs. Decentralized Structure:	

The authors (Gilley and Eggland, 1987) have posited that the mission suggests where the program is "coming from" while objectives and goals indicate where it is going. It is these objectives and goals that provide the superstructure for the remainder of the marketing plan.

HRD program objectives can vary from year to year depending on the problems or topics the program must address. However, the purpose of each objective should be to accomplish the broader mission of the program. HRD practitioners who fail to filter their objectives through the mission will discover themselves off course and will awaken to the realization that they are engaging in activities they were not intended or qualified to accomplish. Each organization has its major objectives that are responsive to its mission; the HRD objectives and subsequent marketing objectives should follow in line with that broader set. For every organization, too, there is always a potential set of relative objectives. This is, of course, true of the HRD department and specifically of its marketing function. It is the task of the HRD marketing planner to make choices among those potential objectives, which might be to deliver more training, to deliver more efficient training, to increase the array or variety of clients or employees served by the HRD department, to use more public information devices so that the HRD department becomes well known, or a variety of others.

Again the organization's major objectives can vary. Major marketing objectives can vary from year to year depending on the perception of major problems that exist within the HRD department, and that must be addressed at the time. We have suggested (Gilley and Eggland, 1989) that the chosen objectives must be related in an operational, continuous, and measurable form. When this is done, they become goals. For example, an objective to "increase enrollment" must be converted into a goal, such as "a 20 percent enrollment increase among first-line supervisors during the first quarter." A goal statement allows HRD practitioners to prepare, plan, control, and allocate financial and human resources as a means of accomplishing the program's objectives. By establishing marketing goals, HRD marketing planners are determining not only if the objectives are feasible but who was responsible and accountable for accomplishing the objectives, and what strategies and activities should be used. Each of these questions must be addressed when deciding whether to adopt a proposed goal. Once a set of goals is agreed upon, HRD marketing planners are ready to examine and determine the most appropriate market for the program.

It will not be possible to identify or complete all goals. Typically, an organization will evaluate a large set of potential goals to examine their consistency with each other. An evaluation is also necessary to determine if the HRD mission has been adhered to. They may discover that they cannot simultaneously achieve a 20 percent enrollment during the first quarter as well as reduce expenses by 10 percent. In this case, the marketing planner may make adjustments in the target level or target dates or drop certain goals altogether in order to arrive at a meaningful and achievable set of goals. Once the set of goals is agreed upon in the formulation stage, the organization is ready to move on to the detailed work of strategy formulation.

There are two problems associated with goal development. The first of these is when different groups within the organization have different marketing goals. The HRD department may have goals that differ from the marketing goals embraced by the parent organization. This glitch should be teased out and remedied during the analytical stage that precedes goal setting. A second problem that sometimes occurs is when organizations have stated and unstated goals that differ from one another. For instance, they may say that their marketing goal is to increase market share, while their real marketing goal is to increase their gross margin. These two goals require somewhat different positioning on the part of the organization in general and the HRD department in particular, and the conflict between them must be solved before progress can be made.

Conclusion

Strategic marketing planning begins with the identification of a mission statement. Such a statement can help HRD practitioners develop a better focus for their program. It can also serve as a way of directing the program and assisting in the allocation of limited financial and human resources.

HRD practitioners must also conduct internal and external analyses to determine their strengths, weaknesses, opportunities, and constraints. The analyses can also reveal critical events and/or trends that might impact HRD.

Finally, HRD practitioners must develop their programs, goals, and objectives, which will provide the HRD staff with targets to achieve. Goals and objectives can also be used to measure the impact of HRD, which should be communicated to upper management and organizational decision makers.

Once the HRD market planner has completed the first three steps of the strategic marketing planning process—that is, developing the mission, examining the attendant environments, and setting objectives and goals—the things learned at those earlier stages must be integrated into a long-term strategy for marketing. In other words, the opportunities and threats in the external environment must be compared to the organization's strengths and weaknesses in order to determine what long-term course of marketing action for the HRD department will best achieve what management has communicated are its real mission and objectives.

Chapter Five

Market Research and Segmentation: Offering the Right Program at the Right Time

There are two concepts that must be subscribed to by any HRD program serious about using marketing. They are market research and market segmentation.

If an HRD group adopts the marketing concept and all that it implies—namely, that a marketing-oriented organization must be constantly working to determine and fulfill the needs of clients— then it follows that the organization in question must know as much as possible about these clients. The main means by which this will occur is market research.

The day has passed when HRD programs were able to develop training programs and/or services, naively introduce them to a mass market, and expect to "get lucky with a portion of the market." Today, the only viable strategy for hitting a target market is to engage in the careful process of market segmentation. These two concepts, market research and market segmentation, are inextricably interwoven. They will be treated in some detail in this chapter.

Market Research for Human Resource Development

As was implied earlier, the best marketer is the one who knows most about the market. The way to know about it intimately and scientifically is through the process of *market research*. Market research is the orderly acquisition and analysis of data that measure some component of a marketing system for the purpose of improving an organization's marketing decisions. Such research can be very diverse. It can involve conducting one-time field research, analyzing data provided by internal record systems or by secondary sources of information, or conducting experiments, surveys, focus groups, interviews, and a myriad of other research strategies. It differs from simple observation and common sense in that it is planned and is tied to specific decision-making situations (Kotler and Andreasen, 1987).

Although they often do good needs analysis, HRD departments tend to do very little market research. This is a result of their reluctance to adopt marketing methods as well as of their limited budgets and research skill. Motivating them to do market research as part of the marketing planning strategy calls for both education and understanding. Showing organizational executives what market research can do for the organization generally and the human resource development department specifically, teaching them how to do it properly, and encouraging them to do it more often are all important aspects of an HRD manager's job.

What are the constraints on initiating market research?

There are several constraints that keep managers from encouraging or allowing HRD practitioners to do market research.

- *Market research is often considered necessary only for decisions involving large amounts of money.* In such cases, the consensus is that it should always be carried out. But market research should also be viewed from a cost-benefit perspective. The costs are usually of two varieties: research expenses, including data collection, data analysis, and so forth; and the amount of sales or competitive advantage lost by delaying a decision until the results are in. The benefits are measured in terms of improvements in the marketing decision that is under consideration. The value of the improvement, in turn, is a function of the stakes involved and how certain the managers are about the rightness of the contemplated decision.
- *The current wisdom is that all market research is survey research.* Surveys can have costs in the thousands of dollars and

sometimes result in findings of limited value. They consume time as well and are not always the appropriate strategy to employ. But to rule out all market research on these grounds is wisdom misplaced. The company might instead try test marketing in a representative market, a strategy that would reduce costs and yield useful data. Another low-cost approach would be to commission focus group interviews of eight to twelve members of the target audience at a time. Although the results are not strictly inferable to a larger market because the groups are not randomly selected, these results can cut the costs of a survey by a quarter or a half.

- *Executives feel that market research always costs a great deal of money.* We have already seen that there are often low-cost alternatives to the kinds of field surveys most HRD managers normally consider. To be knowledgeable users of market research, managers must know how and when to do traditional survey research, and how and when to use a wide range of low-cost techniques as alternatives.
- *Some feel that a high level of methodological sophistication is essential in market research.* True, one who does market research needs to be fundamentally acquainted with such concepts as research design and samplings, or have access to someone who is, but in-depth knowledge is not necessary.
- *Experience or hearsay leads some to believe that research results are frequently not used.* This belief can be counteracted by making certain that research is initiated after the management has made clear to the HRD market researchers what the decision alternatives are, and what it is about those decisions that necessitates additional information. It also helps if the relationship between the results in the decision is clearly understood and the results are communicated well (Kotler and Andreasen, 1987).

How does an HRD professional do market research?

As a reinforcement, market research and systematic gathering of data increase the probability of successful marketing in the HRD department. Research findings are essential to planning and developing marketing strategies. Information about markets provides vital input in planning the marketing mix and in controlling marketing activities. The marketing concept can be better implemented when adequate information about customers or clients is available.

The real value of market research and the systematic gathering of information that supports it is measured by improvements and a marketer's ability to make decisions. Research and the information that it develops provide feedback from customers and clients to the organization. Without this feedback, an HRD marketer cannot understand the dynamics of the marketplace. Just as public opinion polls provide political leaders with quick feedback about voters' feelings, market research can provide the HRD organization with insights regarding the desires of clients. Marketing strategies will be directly influenced by the opinions voiced through market research.

The HRD organization should have effective methods of determining when research is needed, and its marketing specialists should be able to plan projects that will provide useful information to decision makers. Practical and understandable procedures should guide the research effort and provide a framework for its completion. Most importantly, HRD marketers must take a logical approach to market research in order to maintain the control necessary to provide adequate data. Market research follows the five steps that every junior high school student learned as the "scientific method." This method has been successfully applied to research in social sciences generally and to market research specifically.

The steps are identifying and defining the problem, developing hypotheses, collecting data, interpreting the findings, and developing the research report. They should be viewed as a guide rather than as a rigid set of rules to be followed in each market research activity. HRD marketers must think about how each of the five steps can best be tailored to fit a particular marketing problem. The following sections look at these steps more closely.

Identifying and Defining the Problem. One of the most difficult things for the HRD marketer to do is to define the problem in specific terms. Many times marketing problems are elusive in their nature and seemingly quite global. Problem refining and definition is the first step toward launching a research study or finding a solution. Decreasing sales, increasing expenses, or decreases in prof-its are frequently broad indications of problems. However, to iden-tify the specific causes through research, marketers must define the scope of the problem and develop problem definitions that go beyond surface symptoms.

According to Gilley (1990), some techniques that HRD mar-keters may consider for pinpointing specific problems include

- Study the firm's records and reports
- Carefully observe processes in the organization
- Have relevant talks with other qualified persons in the organi-zation
- Carefully observe and study the procedures and techniques of the most efficient and successful firms in the industry
- Read pertinent published materials
- Use check-lists to evaluate the firm's operations
- Use "brainstorming," that is, intensified discussions with a group of interested persons.

Developing Hypotheses. A hypothesis is a guess or assumption as-sociated with a problem. More specifically, it is a guess as to the solution of the problem that is to be tested in the market research process. The guess is based on all the insight and knowledge avail-able to the HRD marketer about the problem from previous research studies and general information. Sometimes several hypotheses are developed in the course of a market research study. The ones that are accepted or rejected become the chief conclusions drawn from the study.

Hypotheses are normally stated as directional or null. An ex-ample of a directional hypothesis would be: *Increasing the amount of time spent on training for stress reduction in the organization will reduce the number of cardiovascular related illnesses experienced by the organization's employees.* The null version of this hypothesis (meaning no difference between or among variables) would read as follows: *It is not known whether increasing the number of hours of stress reduction training will decrease, increase, or not affect the number of cardiovascular related illnesses among the organization's employees.* In the case of the directional hypothesis, if it is accepted, then the conclusion is that increasing the amount of time spent in stress reduction will result in fewer illnesses.

Collecting Data. Having defined the problem and developed hypotheses, the HRD marketers need to collect data and information to support or refute their working conclusions. Both primary and secondary data are available to them. *Primary data* are observed and recorded or collected directly from respondents. *Secondary data* are compiled inside or outside the organization for purposes only secondarily related to the current investigation. Examples of secondary data include general reports supplied by various data services concerning market shares, retail inventory levels, and consumer purchasing behavior. Primary data, in contrast, must be gathered by developing a method to either observe the phenomenon or survey respondents.

The nature and type of hypotheses being tested will help to determine which general data gathering approaches or research strategies to use. There are several schemes for categorizing the various types of research and many good market research resources will differ on their merits. The one we have chosen is to simply categorize market research as either descriptive or experimental.

Descriptive research strategies involve strategies designed to determine the current status of a subject, topic, event, idea, and/or phenomenon. They include surveys, whether by mail, telephone, or personal interview, and a variety of other methods. Only four such strategies will be reviewed here.

1. Mail surveys. Here, questionnaires are sent to respondents who are encouraged to complete and return them. This approach is used most often when the individuals chosen for questioning are spread over a wide area and funds for the survey are limited. Mail surveys are the least expensive method if the response rate is high enough to produce reliable results; their main disadvantage is that response rates may in fact be low. A high rate usually is attained with highly motivated respondents such as regular customers, organization members, or people who are hard to interview but have an interest in the topic. Results may be misleading, however, if respondents are significantly different from the population being sampled. Sometimes premiums or incentives are used to encourage

respondents to return questionnaires. This approach has been effective in developing panels of respondents who are interviewed repeatedly by mail.

2. Telephone surveys. These require respondents to answer questionnaires administered by interviewers. A telephone survey has some advantages over a mail survey. The rate of response is higher because it is usually easier for respondents to cooperate; it takes less effort to answer the telephone and talk than to fill out a questionnaire. Also, if enough interviewers are used, a telephone survey can be conducted very quickly. Political candidates or organizations seeking an immediate reaction may use telephone surveys for this very reason. Their limitations are that they are limited to oral communication; visual aids or observation cannot be included; and interpretation of results must make adjustments for subjects who are not at home and for those without telephones.

3. Personal interviews. This method has traditionally been used by market researchers because of its flexibility. Another advantage is that various audiovisual aids can be used in the course of the interview. Moreover, direct interaction usually permits more in-depth interviewing and, because face-to-face interviews can be longer, more information can be gathered through them. Finally, respondents can be selected more carefully and topics can be explored more thoroughly.

4. Focus-group interviews. One method for collecting primary data without a survey is the focus-group interview. Here groups rather than individuals are interviewed. The object is to observe group interaction when members are exposed to an idea or concept. Groups of eight to twelve target consumers, usually (but not always) a relatively homogeneous group, are brought together to discuss a specific set of issues under the guidance of a leader trained to stimulate and focus the discussion. Although the results of focus groups are frequently not projectable to the population in a scientific fashion, they can often provide rich insights into consumer perceptions and preferences regarding a product, service, or organization. They are particularly useful as a means of testing product concepts and proposed advertisements, package design, posters, instructions, instructional programs, and so forth. Finally, they are useful in generating lists of factors to consider in more

elaborate field studies and so are often part of the developmental phase of major research programs.

A major problem with survey research is that it relies on information volunteered by consumers. The quality of the measurements can well be compromised by interviewee or interviewer bias. Many private organizations have sought to develop more objective behavioral measures through *experimental research strategies*. Experimental opportunities abound. Too many HRD organizations could learn about their marketplace by, for instance, applying different marketing strategies to different subsamples of the target population, but fail to do so.

Finding out which variables cause an event to occur may be difficult if researchers do not adopt an experimental approach. Experimentation involves maintaining as constant those factors that are related to or may affect the variables under investigation so that the effects of the experimental variables may be measured.

In the experimental approach, *independent variables* (those variables free from the influence of, or not dependent on, other variables) are usually manipulated in order to measure relationships or changes in a *dependent variable* (a variable contingent on or restricted to one or a set of values assumed by the independent variable) (Gilley, 1991). For example, an HRD manager in setting the price of a new instructional program may want to estimate the number of enrollees that could be attracted at various prices. The dependent variable would be sales, and the independent variable would be price. Researchers would design the experiment so that other independent variables that might influence sales—such as advertising, distribution, and variation of the product—would be controlled variables. Experiments might be conducted in a laboratory or in a field. Each setting would have its advantages and disadvantages.

As an aid to market decision making, experimentation is used in research design to improve hypothesis testing. But whether experiments are conducted in the laboratory or in the field, many assumptions have to be made so that the number of factors can be limited and causal factors can be isolated. Marketing decision makers must recognize that these assumptions may limit the reliability of research findings.

Interpreting Research Findings. Having collected data to test their hypotheses, HRD marketers are now ready to interpret the research findings. Interpretation will be easier if marketers carefully plan their data analysis methods early in the research process. They should also try to allow for continual evaluation of the data throughout the collection period, since this procedure will give them insight into areas that should be probed during the formal interpretation.

First the HRD market researcher must tabulate the data. If the objective is to understand the results as they apply to individual categories of things or people being studied, then cross-tabulation might be quite useful, especially in tabulating joint occurrences. This usually involves the development of a matrix that has categories stated along each axis with figures filling the cells. Table 5.1 provides an example of a cross-tabulation matrix developed by an HRD market researcher in looking for reasons why people attended a stress-reduction workshop.

After the data have been tabulated they must be analyzed. Statistical interpretation focuses on what is typical or what deviates from the average. It indicates how widely respondents vary and how they are distributed in relation to the variable being measured. This is another aspect of market research in which HRD marketers must use judgments or intuition. When interpreting statistics, marketers

Table 5.1. Reasons for Attending a Stress-Reduction Workshop, by Age, in Order of Frequency.

		Age	
Reasons	*Under 40*	*41–55*	*56–65*
1. Current heart problems	30%	35%	45%
2. History of heart problems	25	30	35
3. Health conscious	15	15	5
4. Interpersonal difficulties	15	10	5
5. Drug or alcohol dependence	10	5	5
6. Curiosity	5	5	5
Total	100%	100%	100%

Source: William M. Mercer, Inc. Reprinted with permission.

rely on estimates of expected error or deviation from the true values of the population.

Developing the Research Report. The final step in the market research process is preparing a report of the research findings. The analysis of data may lead researchers to accept or reject the hypotheses that were stated early in the study. Usually, results are communicated in a formal written report and time must be allowed for this when planning and scheduling the project. Since the purpose of the report is to communicate with the decision makers who must use the research findings, researchers also should consider how much detail and supporting data to include in the report. Often if the decision makers do not have time to get involved in understanding how the results were obtained, the researchers will state their summary and recommendations first. However, a technical report does allow its users to analyze data and interpret recommendations, since it also describes the research methods and procedures and at least the most important data gathered.

Market research for the HRD effort is important to the organization's marketing planning activity. The marketing concept cannot be implemented without information about clients or customers. Market research involves a scientific approach to decision making in marketing for HRD. Intuitive managers make decisions on the basis of past experience and personal bias, but decision making that makes use of research is done in an orderly, logical, and systematic way. Although minor, nonrecurrent marketing problems can be handled successfully by intuition, as the number of possible solutions increases and the risks become greater an approach that involves research is more rewarding and desirable.

Market Segmentation for HRD

The next major concept to consider while preparing to develop a marketing plan for HRD is *market segmentation.* The first step in determining the most appropriate market—the *target market,* as it is called—is to understand the term "market." A market is a universe of people who have an actual or potential interest in a product or service and the ability to pay for that product or service. When examined more closely, every market is heterogeneous, that is, it is made up of quite different types of consumers or *market segments*.

Why should HRD professionals segment their market?

The theory of market segmentation is based on the fact that client or customer preferences are often clustered. Some people, for instance, will be satisfied only with a custom-tailored HRD program and can pay the high cost, whereas most people would be very satisfied with the less expensive program aimed at a broader market. Segmentation procedures can reveal the existence of natural market segments, or can be used to construct market segments, or can reveal the lack of any market segments.

How are HRD markets segmented?

Typically, three kinds of variables are used in segmenting consumer markets: geographical, demographic, and behavioristic. The choice of variables for market segmentation will, of course, depend upon the problem the HRD department is seeking to clarify.

Geographical Segmentation. In geographical segmentation the market is divided by location, which may be as large as a nation or as small as a neighborhood, on the assumption that consumers' needs and preferences vary by where they live. Geographical segmentation may be appropriate when an HRD department wishes to develop differentiated brochures and client recruitment plans for various regions of the country. Knowing where prospects live may tell the department some useful things about what the clients are seeking in a program and what aspects of the program would be most appealing to them.

Demographic Segmentation. Here, the market is divided into groups based on demographic variables such as age, sex, family size, family life cycle, income, occupation, education, religion, race, and nationality. Demographic variables are the most frequently used segmentation variables for three reasons. First, consumer wants, preferences, and usage rates are often highly associated with demographic variables. Second, demographic variables are easier to define and measure than are most other segmentation variables. Third, even when the desired target market is described in terms of other nondemographic variables, reaching that market will depend upon how familiar the practitioner is with the characteristics of the market and the media it uses.

Behavioristic Segmentation. Sometimes marketers are particularly interested in how consumers respond to an actual program or service, rather than in their general life-style or personality. Many marketers believe that behavioristic variables are the best starting point for constructing useful market segments, because behavior has direct implications for which programs client segments will choose.

Target Marketing

Segmenting the market helps HRD professionals identify the opportunities facing their program. Now the HRD professional must decide what kind of a targeting strategy will be used with the product or program that is to be delivered. There are three broad strategies that should be considered: undifferentiated marketing, differentiated marketing, and concentrated marketing.

Undifferentiated Marketing. Undifferentiated marketing is another name for mass marketing. In this approach, the organization chooses to ignore the different market segments and instead focuses on consumers' common needs. Since it designs one program that will appeal to the largest number of clients, it is the marketing counterpart of standardization and mass production in manufacturing. And like these, it is dependent on reduced unit costs, such as material development and instructional design time. Lower costs, however, are frequently accompanied by reduced client satisfaction as the program fails to meet varying individual needs.

Differentiated Marketing. A program using differentiated marketing operates in two or more segments of the market but designs separate programs for each segment. The organization using this approach can anticipate better results than one using undifferentiated marketing. However, since the organization has to spend more on marketing research, product-program development, communications, and other tasks, it needs to balance the likelihood of greater effect against higher cost before deciding whether to adopt differentiated marketing.

Concentrated Marketing. Concentrated marketing is a special case of differentiated marketing in which the organization segments the market and then selects one segment as the focus of its marketing efforts. The organization concentrates on serving that one segment well, hoping to achieve the following benefits:

- A strong following and standing in a particular market segment
- Greater knowledge of the market segment's needs and behavior
- Operating economies in product distribution and promotion

Concentrated marketing may involve higher-than-normal risks in that the selected market segment may decline or disappear.

For example, in a large insurance company, the target market for its HRD program would be the administrative personnel, insurance agents, underwriters, regional sales managers, and corporate executives, taken together. Taken individually, each of these job classifications is a market segment, each with a different degree of interest in the organization. The HRD practitioners within this organization would benefit by constructing a market segmentation scheme that would reveal the characteristics of each of these groups. From this they could decide whether to try to serve all of the segments through an undifferentiated target marketing strategy or to concentrate on a few more promising ones (that is, decide between differentiated marketing and concentrated marketing).

In addition to being segmented by interest in the product or service, a market could also be segmented by variables such as age, sex, educational level, geographic location, and life-style. To continue our example, suppose the HRD practitioners decided to examine an HRD market segmentation scheme for the insurance company. There are five job classifications (market segments): administrative personnel, insurance agents, underwriters, regional sales managers, and corporate executives. There are also five types of training (products): human relations training, computer skills, management skills development, principles of insurance, and sales training. These segments are illustrated in Figure 5.1. In addition, there are also five basic patterns of market coverage. Figure 5.2 illustrates the patterns, along with five alternative approaches to marketing HRD in the insurance company.

Figure 5.1. Segmentation of an Insurance Company by HRD Product.

MARKET

PRODUCT	Administrative Personnel (M1)	Insurance Agents (M2)	Underwriters (M3)	Regional Sales Managers (M4)	Corporate Executives (M5)
Human Relations (P1)					
Computer Skills (P2)					
Management Skills (P3)					
Insurance Principles (P4)					
Sales Training (P5)					

Source: J. W. Gilley and S. A. Eggland. "Hook, Line and Sinker." *Training and Development Journal,* 1987, 41(9), pp. 22–29. Reprinted with permission from the American Society for Training and Development.

Figure 5.2. Five Patterns of Market Coverage in an Insurance Company.

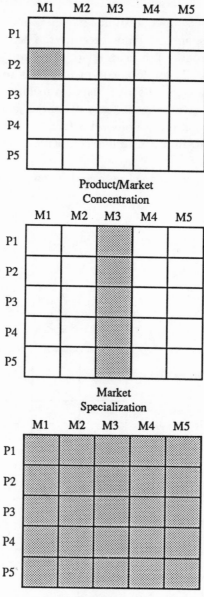

Product/Market
Concentration

Market
Specialization

Full Coverage

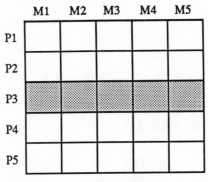

Product
Specialization

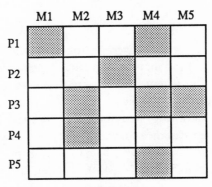

Selective
Specialization

1. *Product/market concentration:* The HRD program concentrates on only one segment (computer skills for administrative personnel).
2. *Product specialization:* The HRD program decides to offer only one product to all of the markets (management skills).
3. *Market specialization:* The HRD program decides to service only one of the market segments (underwriters) with all of the training products.
4. *Selective specializations:* The HRD program tailors its product offerings in such a way as to meet the specialized needs of each market segment.
5. *Full coverage:* The HRD program offers all products to all market segments.

These patterns of coverage, together with the product (HRD training courses) and market segments (job classifications) comprise the segmentation scheme. HRD practitioners use the scheme to decide which approach to take.

After examining each of the five alternatives, the HRD practitioners in the insurance company must decide which one will best accomplish the objectives and goals of the program and remain consistent with its overall mission. In some circumstances a combination of equally attractive alternatives might be selected.

HRD marketers who carefully delineate and examine their markets are bound to have greater success in getting their programs accepted and moving toward the achievement of their organizational mission.

Conclusion

Strategic marketing planning should have a foundation in solid market research, which can offer HRD practitioners a number of benefits. It can provide needed information about the organization's human resources, its growth opportunities, and its clients' attitudes toward HRD. This and other data gathered from market research is useful when deciding how to allocate resources. Market research can also help identify specific trends, which can allow HRD practitioners to adjust their focus in order to better serve the organization.

Market segmentation can help practitioners determine which clients need specific training programs and services, and can offer evidence on the depth and breadth of a population and its interest in training. This involves finding out as much as possible about the market that is to be served and then developing a market segmentation strategy designed to minister specifically to the unique needs of each of the clients.

Chapter Six

Setting Program Priorities and Allocating Limited Resources

Having identified the most appropriate audience, our next task as strategic marketing planners is to identify the marketing mix. The marketing mix consists of four kinds of strategies designed to help the HRD program accomplish its goals and objectives: program/ service strategy, cost-benefit strategy, time-location strategy, and promotional strategy. This chapter focuses its attention on the program/service strategy. We will begin, then, by determining the nature of HRD programs and services.

The first thing to be said about HRD programs and services is that they are both *products*. Ferrell and Pride (1982) have defined a product as anything that one receives during an exchange. A product may be a good, service, or idea. Products consist of tangible and intangible attributes. Warmke and Palmer (1985) have pointed out that when people purchase a product, they are purchasing not only the product itself but also the benefits it yields. In other words, people purchase products for what they will do for them. Therefore, we can conclude that a product is any item that can be exchanged for the purpose of receiving benefits.

In Chapter Two, we identified several possible types of benefits—sensory, psychic, place, time, and monetary—that can be received from an exchange. We also stated that the most common benefits in HRD are psychic and monetary. In HRD, the products exchanged for benefits include training programs and HRD services.

HRD clients select training programs and services that improve performance problems and satisfy developmental needs. Therefore HRD practitioners must make certain that each and every training program and service product offered is directed at a performance problem or developmental need. This will ensure increased participation in training programs as well as increased usage of services. Another outcome of appropriate offerings is increased client satisfaction and reduced cognitive dissonance.

How to Classify Training Programs and HRD Services

Training programs and HRD services are classified as *consumer goods*. This means they are selected or used by people for their personal use. Consumer goods are further classified according to how they are selected by HRD clients. This is extremely important from a marketing standpoint. The classification of training programs and HRD services also dictates how HRD practitioners promote them, how often they are made available, and the type of cost-benefit strategy employed. Training programs and HRD services are subclassified into convenience goods, shopping goods, and specialty goods.

Convenience Goods

HRD convenience goods, according to Barry (1986), are ones that

- Require little or no effort to select or use
- Maintain a low involvement
- Are selected or used frequently
- Maintain a perceived low risk

An example of convenience goods would be training aids that are designed to reinforce knowledge, skills, or attitudes. Such aids are often given to clients during or after training programs. They require little or no effort to use. They also do not require direct involvement by the HRD practitioner except as a means of reminding the client of the concepts taught or skills learned. Other examples of convenience goods are breakfast and luncheon seminars, on-the-job training activities for low-skills related occupations, and structured self-study programs. Each of these training programs meets the criteria previously identified.

The first marketing effort should be to make convenience goods as widely available as possible, to maximize their exposure to and use by clients. This is essential because the customer does not actively search for convenience goods.

Shopping Goods

Barry characterizes HRD shopping goods as products that

- Require extensive effort to select
- Maintain a moderate to high cost to design and develop
- Require a high information search
- Are selected infrequently
- Maintain moderate to high perceived risk

HRD shopping goods are the heart of HRD programs and are the principal reason HRD programs exist. Training programs are the primary shopping goods offered by HRD programs.

Shopping goods require much more time and effort to select than convenience products. This is because shopping goods are selected by HRD clients to solve a performance problem or satisfy a developmental need. As a result, clients will spend the time needed to investigate possible training programs. Shopping goods are also much more risky than convenience goods. For example, a training program that does not improve performance or satisfy developmental needs will be of little value to clients. Further, it will bring about dissatisfaction with the HRD program and its practitioners. At the same time, HRD clients and the organization stand to lose valuable time and effort on such training programs. The three-way exchange process outlined in Chapter Two illustrated this principle. Poorly designed and developed training programs can cause many problems: 1. Loss of credibility on the part of the HRD program and its practitioners; 2. Loss of production time while attending training programs; 3. Development of improper knowledge and skills;

4. Development of improper and/or inappropriate attitudes; 5. Loss of improved productivity and efficiency; 6. Loss of improved profitability.

HRD practitioners should begin their marketing efforts by identifying the characteristics of their training programs and services and the benefits that each has to offer HRD clients. This will ensure they are based upon the performance problems and developmental needs identified and desired by clients. In addition, HRD practitioners should pay close attention to the cost-benefit relationship of each training program and service. The location/time strategy and promotional strategy employed by HRD practitioners must be carefully considered for shopping goods. Finally, for every training program and service offered, HRD practitioners should seriously evaluate two features provided in the latter part of this chapter: the concept life cycle and the portfolio analysis model. This will help them allocate limited resources.

Specialty Goods

Barry's definition of HRD specialty goods are products that require

- Unlimited effort to select
- High design and development cost
- Low information search
- Low frequency of selection
- High perceived risk

This type of product is generally selected because a serious performance problem has emerged or an organizational development issue is seriously impacting the organization. Specialty goods are the sort to require unique skills and talented individuals to facilitate change. Because of the specialized nature of performance problems and a limited number of qualified individuals to address such problems, a low information search is required.

Specialty goods normally come in the form of a service rather than a tangible product. In many organizations, external HRD professionals are hired to deliver such services. They generally work with or through the internal HRD practitioners and directly with members of the organization. They are therefore viewed as agents of the HRD program. As a result, their efforts are a direct reflection on the HRD program, its reputation, and image.

Services classified as specialty products should be further classified in order to better understand them, and thus become better able to manage them. They should be examined according to the nature of the service, the relationship with members of the client group, and the method(s) of service delivery (Barry, 1986). These three subclassifications will not only enable HRD practitioners to better categorize services but help them allocate resources.

Improving Training Programs and Services

Every training program and service begins as an idea before it is developed into an actual program. We refer to this as the *product development process.* It consists of five stages: idea generation, idea screening, training program and service planning and development, pilot testing, and implementation.

Idea Generation

Some estimates indicate that as many as 100 ideas are necessary for every successful training program and/or service. While this is an average figure it serves to illustrate the complexity of training program and service development as well as the high mortality rate of ideas. In HRD, the process of idea generation begins with the identification of a performance problem or developmental need. Such problems and needs must be the basis of program and services development. Therefore, idea generation begins with appropriate needs assessment procedures.

However, to obtain as many good ideas as possible, it is also necessary to establish a system by which ideas can be generated and recorded. One such way is to create a network of individuals interested in the creation of potential HRD programs and services. This should include centers of influence, executives, managers, supervisors, and key employees who can produce ideas and share them with HRD practitioners for further screening. One of the best ways of facilitating this process is to develop an advisory committee. It should consist of managers, supervisors, executives, and employees. The committee can serve the HRD program by reviewing training programs and services and participating in front-end analyses and needs assessments.

An advisory committee can provide HRD programs with an invaluable network that can be used to communicate the value of HRD to others in the organization. Members of such a committee become the internal advocates of HRD. They will market HRD for you and help you acquire needed funding and political support.

Idea Screening

The principal purpose of the screening stage is to identify ideas (needs) that have potential for conversion into training programs or services. A team of HRD practitioners and several members of the client group should participate in this process. This will ensure that all factions of the organization are represented. It will also provide management a way to react to ideas generated and to analyze and evaluate their potential effects.

Ideas may be eliminated for several reasons:

- Irrelevance: they are outside the mission of HRD.
- Expense: the costs of prevention exceed the benefits obtained.
- Risk: they seem likely to have a negative impact on the organization.
- Image: the training program or services are not positively affecting the image of HRD.
- Resources: the HRD program does not possess the financial or human resources to adequately develop them.
- Skills: the HRD practitioners do not have the specialized knowledge or skills required to address them.

Ideas that are accepted as legitimate are considered for further research and development.

Training Program and Service Planning and Development

In this stage, ideas are completely evaluated. The process begins with the appointment of a project manager who will be responsible for the development of an idea into a training program or service. Each training program or service should be analyzed according to its potential, its impact, its costs, its benefits, and its longevity. The financial and human resources required to produce and deliver a training program or service should also be determined. The clients' initial reaction to the training program or services is another important consideration. Their insight is invaluable to the development of effective and impact-oriented training programs and services. Therefore, it is critical that HRD practitioners obtain their initial reaction before the planning and development phase.

Project managers should develop a project plan that identifies every activity required to produce the training program in its final form. The plan should also include the amount of time required to complete each activity. The activities should be priorities, beginning with the activity that must be completed first and followed in order by subsequent ones. In Exhibit 6.1, we have provided a sample of a project plan used to complete a time management program at William M. Mercer, Incorporated. We have identified thirteen separate but related tasks that must be completed in order to design, develop, and implement a time management training program. For each task, a specific time line has been determined from the beginning of the task until its completion. Some tasks must be completed sequentially; others can be completed simultaneously. Every task is listed and appropriate time frames are highlighted.

Pilot Testing a Training Program or Service

In this stage, HRD practitioners attempt to solicit client reaction to a training program or service under actual training conditions. As the process begins, the practitioners must identify levels of expectation for the training programs or services during the testing period. This will help determine the success or failure of a training program or service during the pilot.

In order to determine future reactions, it is very important that a representative sample of clients be identified for the pilot. The sample participants can provide accurate feedback to HRD practitioners regarding the value of the training programs or services. For example, if a training program in delegation skills is being piloted, a representative sample of managers and supervisors who would ultimately participate in such a program must be included in the pilot. This will ensure accurate information regarding the effectiveness of learning activities, appropriateness of instructional methods, value of the program's outcome, and applicability of concepts learned. This information should serve as feedback to the project manager for integration into the program design before final development.

Another purpose of a pilot is to determine if the training program or service under consideration provides the value and benefits expected. Therefore, it is important that the pilot be realistic. For example, additional training activity and exercises that are not available in the normal program should not be allowed during the pilot test. The training program or service must be tested in everyday situations to determine its appeal as well as its usefulness.

Implementation

Once a pilot has been successfully completed, the training program or service is ready for full-scale introduction to its potential audience. At this point, the concept life cycle begins for HRD products. Therefore, it is time to focus on the characteristics of training programs and services as they move through their life cycle.

The Concept Life Cycle

Every training program and service, regardless of type, goes through a life cycle. This cycle consists of four stages: exposure, acceptance, maturity, and decline (see Figure 6.1). It is known as the *concept life cycle* (Gilley and Eggland, 1989; Gilley, 1987). Some training programs move through this life cycle at a very rapid rate; others require much more time to pass through all four stages. The rapidity with which a learning program or training activity will move through the cycle is dependent on its importance and practical application.

The concept life cycle differs for each training program and service. This is because the adoption rate and longevity are different for each. The adoption of some training programs and services

Exhibit 6.1. Program Management: Typical Training Program Design.

TASK	April 14	15	16	17	May 18	19	20	21	June 22	23
Conduct Need Analysis and Task Analysis	■	■	■							
Develop Evaluation Strategies	■	■	■							
Identify Performance Objectives				■	■					
Develop Learning Activities					■	■	■			
Develop Structure and Sequence of Objectives and Activities							■	■		
Identify Institutional Strategies							■	■	■	■
Develop Media, Material, and Training Aids										
Create Lesson Plans										
Create Course Material										
Produce Participant Manuals										
Identify Pilot Group							■	■		
Conduct Pilot Program										
Conduct Evaluation (Reaction)										
(Learning)										
(Impact)										

Source: William M. Mercer, Inc. Reprinted with permission.

		July						August				September			
24	25	26	27	28	29	30	31	32	33	34	35	36	37	38	39

(Three months after intervention)

(Six months after intervention)

Figure 6.1. The Concept Life Cycle.

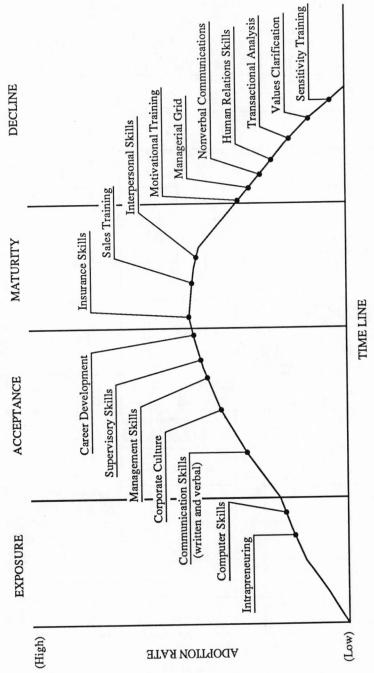

Source: Gilley, 1987, p. 12.

begins very slowly and then rises very rapidly. Some programs never become very popular or useful. Others experience a period of new growth after an extended period of decline, while others appear to be eternal. Figure 6.2 reflects these various life cycle shapes. Regardless of shape, however, the concept life cycle consists of a period of exposure, followed by periods of acceptance, maturity, and decline.

What is the importance of the concept life cycle?

By understanding the concept life cycle and its assumptions, HRD practitioners can better manage their training programs and services through the proper allocation of financial and human resources. Resources of both types are required for the design, development, and implementation of training programs and services. In addition, critical decisions regarding promotional activities, cost-benefit considerations, and the number of offerings made available can be better made if one uses the concept life cycle. For example, training programs and services in the exposure stage will require greater promotional activity than ones in the maturity stage; the frequency of the adoption rate will affect the number of offerings made available; and the higher the adoption rate becomes, the more favorable will be the cost-benefit relationship (assuming costs are proportional).

What are the stages of the concept life cycle?

Figure 6.3 reflects the elements of the concept life cycle and the activities associated with each stage. The figure provides HRD practitioners with a vehicle for critical decision making related to each stage of the life cycle.

Exposure. The exposure stage is the period of time when a training program or service has just been developed. During that period, the number of individuals adopting or utilizing the program or service is very small. In Chapter Three, we identified people who participate during this stage as innovators. They are generally centers of influence who can serve as internal advocates within the organization. Accordingly, this is a very critical period for new training programs or services. The marketing objective during this stage is

**Figure 6.2. Adoption Rates of HRD Programs and Services
Over Time: Four Characteristic Life Cycles.**

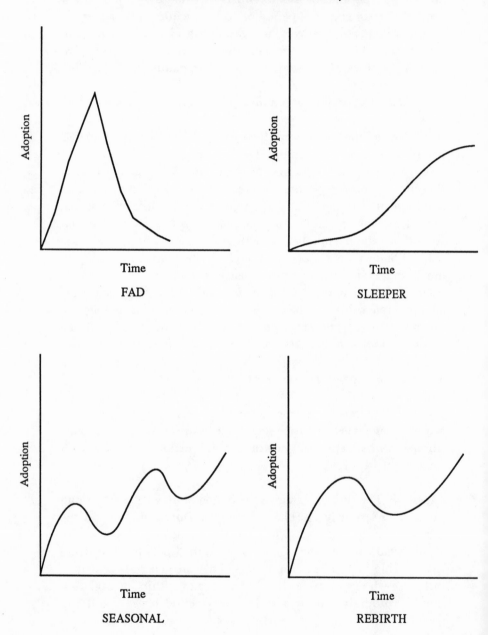

Figure 6.3. Stages in the Concept Life Cycle with Associated Marketing Strategies.

	Stage in Concept Life Cycle			
Element	Exposure	Acceptance	Maturity	Decline
Objective	To get trial.	Establish strong brand position with decision makers and users.	Maintain and strengthen customer loyalty.	Seek remaining benefits.
Competition	None.	Rapid growth, aggressive competition.	Intense. Declining unit benefits, competitors drop out.	Benefits squeeze, fewer competitors.
Product	Few models, high quality.	Modular, flexible, more models for segments merging.	Tighten lines not servicing good markets. Product improvement and differentiation.	Reduce line to major competitors.
Price	Good value.	Long price line from low to premium.	Attention to broadening market.	Maintain levels without regard to share of market.
Promotion	Create awareness, get early trial. Fairly heavy advertising.	Create strong awareness and preference. *Maximum use of mass media.*	Maintain and strengthen consumer. Continue mass media, sales promotion.	Rapid phaseout.
Marketing Research	Discover weaknesses. Identify emerging segments.	Market position, market gaps. Product gaps.	Attention to product improvement. Search for broader market and new promotion themes.	Determine point of product elimination.

to get as many members of the client group as possible to participate in the program or service. It is therefore important to communicate through promotional activities the advantages, benefits, usages, and values of the training program or service.

The cost of researching, designing, and developing training programs and services is very high. HRD practitioners, then, must identify the benefits to be received from participating in training programs and services. In this way, positive value will be perceived by clients. However, this is only one of the problems that practitioners face. If training programs or services fail to be adopted by a sufficient number of clients, the costs incurred will not be covered. We are talking about the level of the adoption rate. As a result of a low rate, training programs or services may fail to progress into the acceptance stage. HRD practitioners must account for this and develop strategies that overcome the client's resistance to the training program or service.

This stage is also characterized by exclusive or selective offerings. This means that training programs or services will be offered only on a limited basis. The reason is that most people are unaware of the program or services and its benefits, so that it does not make sense to offer the program or service too often at this point.

Strategic quality training is an example of a training program that is presently identified as being in the exposure stage of the concept life cycle. Since its introduction in 1990, it has maintained steady interest and adoption by organizations.

Acceptance. As training programs and services begin to be adopted by more and more members of the client group, they enter a period of growth known as the acceptance stage. This is a time in which the programs and services gain acceptance and their benefits and values become more identifiable. This encourages even greater participation and involvement, which gives the programs and services greater chances of success. Early adoptions are common during this stage. During the final phase of this stage, the population will consist of the early majority, which is a sizable proportion of the overall population.

The marketing objective during the acceptance stage is to

establish a strong identity for and awareness of the program. It is therefore essential that the benefits and value of the training program or service be fully communicated to all potential clients within the client group. During this stage, promotional activities should reach their peak.

HRD practitioners should also be very aggressive in the promotion of training programs or services during this period. Announcements of the program or services should be made to the client group. A special offering for centers of influence and key members of the client group should be held. A brochure should be designed, developed, and produced that outlines the program or service and describes the potential benefits of participation. The brochure should then be distributed to all members of the client group who would have an interest in or need for the program or service. The same information should also be included in the HRD program catalog (see Chapter Nine for more information).

Because a larger number of clients participate in training programs or services during the acceptance stage, greater value is generated—often enough to eliminate the initial research, design, and development costs. Once these costs have been eliminated, HRD practitioners can concentrate on generating value to cover the operational costs. It is important to remember that, as a percentage of the overall cost of the program or service, operational costs are generally lower than developmental costs. Combine this with ever-increasing participation, and the cost of each offering of the program or service is significantly reduced. Ultimately, so is the cost of the program or service to the organization. Thus the benefits received are higher in relationship to the cost incurred, an outcome that will encourage even greater participation in the program or service. Consequently, greater awareness of the program's or service's value, plus a better cost-benefit relationship, results in even higher acceptance; and the longer the acceptance stage lasts, the greater the probability that the training program or service will be successful. Finally, the training program or service should now be offered on a more frequent basis than during the exposure stage. The primary reason for this decision is that more clients are now aware of the program or service and its benefits; this will also help to increase its value to the organization and to maximize the value received from it.

It is during the acceptance stage that other departments within the organization begin to consider offering similar training programs or services. For example, the marketing department may feel a need to offer a sales training program to employees. Therefore HRD practitioners will want to make certain that their sales training program is differentiated from the marketing department's. They can accomplish this by identifying the respective differences and communicating the special benefits and values to be received from their version of the program. This will help them develop a competitive niche in relation to other departments.

Project planning, business protocol, personal productivity, and performance management are examples of training programs that are in the acceptance stage of the concept life cycle at William M. Mercer. Each of these programs has existed for an extended period of time and has enjoyed steady adoption and acceptance by members of the client group. One important characteristic of theirs is that they are perceived to be important to the organization and continue to gain acceptance and recognition.

Maturity. When acceptance begins to level off, the training program or service is reaching the maturity stage. In fact, the majority of training programs or services offered by HRD programs are in this stage of matriculation. The late majority are the type of clients that participate during this stage. As a result, the greatest number of clients are ready. The size of the population and the amount of time this stage lasts will ultimately determine the success of the training program or services.

The marketing objective during the maturity stage is to maintain and strengthen participation among the client group. This can be done by continuing promotional activities. The promotional activities that could be used include advisory committee meetings within centers of influence, program announcements, and internal memos designed to remind clients of the program or services through HRD program catalogs and brochures (see Chapter Five for more information).

The training program or services should continue to be offered on a regular basis until attendance per session begins to diminish significantly. The cost-benefit ratio of the training program or service should remain constant during the early phases of this stage. However, adjustments must be made as demand begins to decline. Because of internal competition, HRD practitioners should continue to emphasize the differences in their version of training programs or services. An outcome of this type of communication could be increased participation. As a result, less valuable training programs or services are forced out; the ones that remain can receive additional promotional efforts to capture the interest of the remaining clients.

During the latter period of the maturity stage, interest begins to decline rapidly. HRD practitioners may therefore have to consider alternatives to their training programs or services such as new markets (*market development*), program redesign (*program development*), or enhanced promotional activities to foster increased usage within the current client group (*market penetration*). Figure 6.6, to be discussed later, supplies a review of these concepts.

Situational leadership, interpersonal skills, and quality circles have one thing in common: each has declined in popularity and acceptance during the past few years. Each, however, still remains an important form of training in many organizations. Reduced popularity but positive importance is a principal characteristic of the maturity stage of the concept life cycle.

Decline. The decline stage is reached when interest in a training program or service begins to drop off rapidly. This often occurs with the introduction of a "new" training program or service designed to be a substitute for an existing one. When this occurs, HRD practitioners should consider cutting off promotional activities for the unpopular or unnecessary program or service and make plans for phasing it out.

The marketing objective during this stage is to offer the program or service to laggards among the client group. Laggards often view outdated training programs or services as having proved their worth (see Chapter Three).

Promotional activities should be limited because it may be politically damaging to actively promote a training program or service that most consider outdated. The offerings should also be limited and directed at a very narrow group.

Transactional analysis, values clarification, and sensitivity training are examples of training programs that have reached the extreme end of the concept life cycle. In most organizations, training programs or services of this type have been eliminated because they are no longer perceived as essential for performance improvement.

How can HRD practitioners identify and apply the concept life cycle?

It is very important that HRD practitioners be able to identify which stage a particular training program or service currently occupies. With this knowledge, they can make critical decisions regarding marketing the training program or service. In addition, resources needed to support marketing efforts are expensive and this model can be used to determine their appropriateness and timeliness. The model also communicates that change is unavoidable and preparing for it is essential, since every training program or service will go through each of the four stages of the concept life cycle. Gilley (1987) has identified several criteria that can be used to identify which stage a particular training program or service is at:

1. How important is the training program or service to the organization's performance objectives?
2. What impact will the training program or service have upon client and organizational development?
3. How many research or topical articles have appeared in professional or academic journals in the past two years regarding the training program or service?
4. How many consultants, program providers, book publishers, and academics are currently offering the training program or service?
5. Is the training program or service a topic of discussion at professional meetings or conferences?
6. Is conference time allocated to help HRD practitioners better understand the values and benefits of the training programs or services?

7. Are a number of advertisements appearing in professional journals or through direct mail regarding the training program or service activity?
8. Are new and improved versions of the training program or service now surfacing?

HRD practitioners can utilize the concept life cycle in several ways. First, as we said, they can identify the location in the cycle of a training program or service they are presently using. This will assist HRD practitioners in projecting training programs' and services' future growth and popularity. Second, once practitioners have identified the stage of each training program or service, they can adjust to the adoption of each. This will also help in the allocation of financial and human resources. Third, the concept life cycle can be used in the establishment of decision-making criteria for HRD. This provides HRD practitioners with a way of analyzing the potential of training programs and services and of making decisions regarding the level of support needed. It also provides a way of estimating the value that the organization will receive for HRD.

Portfolio Analysis

While the concept life cycle is an important tool, it does not show the relationship between the relative importance and practical application of training programs or service activities. Therefore, it is important to utilize a second tool, known as *portfolio analysis,* which will be addressed in this section.

How should HRD practitioners use the portfolio analysis?

HRD practitioners can analyze training programs or service activities in terms of either their relative importance or their practical application. In this context, the ones that are perceived as having high relative importance are viewed as being vital and essential in improving performance and satisfying clients' developmental needs. Failure to provide such training programs or service activities could result in an organization's not obtaining its operational results. At the same time, training programs or service activities that

are perceived as having high practical application are ones that
teach concepts, ideas, skills, and behaviors that can be applied to
work settings and/or utilized by members of the client group. When
these criteria are viewed together, a continuum can be constructed
with relative importance and practical application anchored at each
end. However, a realistic evaluation of HRD programs includes both
relative importance and practical application, which thus become
equal partners in the analysis. Therefore, it is inappropriate to ar-
range importance and application along a single continuum. Instead, their working relationship can be illustrated by constructing
two continuums, one horizontal and one vertical. The horizontal
continuum reveals the degree of practical application of programs
or activities while the vertical continuum reveals their relative importance (Figure 6.4). The four primary positions that can be located in this way are here identified as Super Stars, Wandering Stars,
Constant Stars, and No Stars (Gilley, 1987).

Super Stars. This type of training program or service activity is
perceived to be very important and applicable. Programs or services
identified as Super Stars can be considered essential to improving
the performance and satisfying the developmental needs of HRD
clients. HRD practitioners should give utmost attention to these
programs and services as well as greater allocations of financial and
human resources. Super Stars may be considered "hot" nationally
and are used in a number of professional environments (Gilley,
1987). However, it is important to remember that the identification
of program importance and applicability is an individual evaluation; therefore, programs or services may be identified differently in
various settings. Supervisory skills, management skills development, and communication skills (verbal and nonverbal) are examples of programs in the Super Star category.

Wandering Stars. This type of training program or service activity
is perceived to be very important but not very applicable. The principal focus for improvement of these types of training programs or
services by HRD practitioners is applicability. Thus if HRD practitioners can improve the applicability of a Wandering Star program, it can be quickly moved to the Super Star category. Sales

Figure 6.4. Portfolio Analysis of HRD Programs and Service Activities.

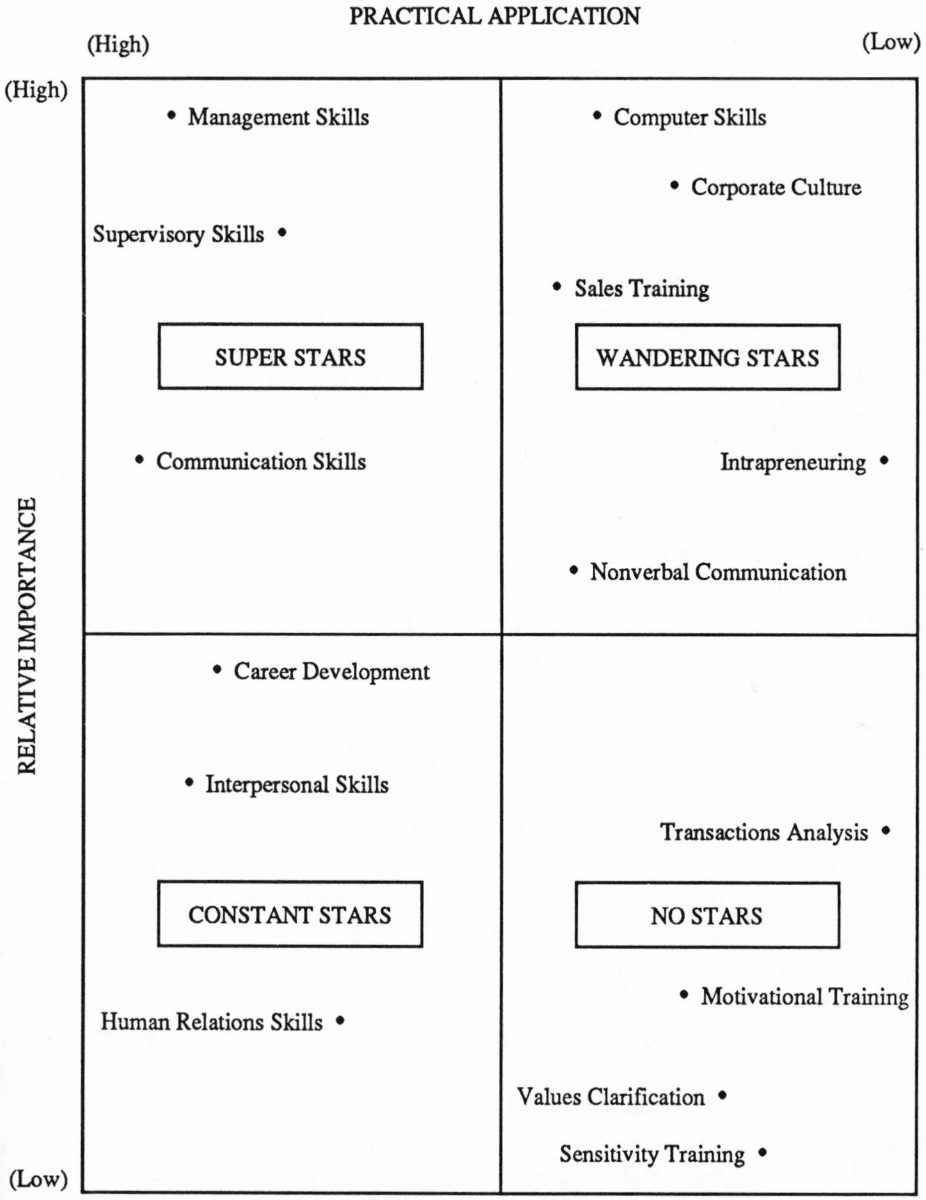

PRACTICAL APPLICATION

(High)   (Low)

(High)

• Management Skills	• Computer Skills
	• Corporate Culture
Supervisory Skills •	
	• Sales Training
SUPER STARS	**WANDERING STARS**
• Communication Skills	Intrapreneuring •
	• Nonverbal Communication
• Career Development	
• Interpersonal Skills	Transactions Analysis •
CONSTANT STARS	**NO STARS**
	• Motivational Training
Human Relations Skills •	Values Clarification •
	Sensitivity Training •

RELATIVE IMPORTANCE

(Low)

Source: Adopted from Gilley, 1987, p. 15.

training, entrepreneurship, computer skills, corporate culture, and nonverbal communication are often identified in this group because it is difficult to apply the concepts learned and to measure accurately the amount of learning that has occurred.

Constant Stars. Training programs or service activities identified in this category are viewed as only moderately important but highly applicable. Since their applicability is high, programs or activities of this type will often exist in large numbers. In fact, this category represents the largest number of training programs and service activities in organizations and HRD practitioners often rely on it to serve as the foundation of their overall HRD program. Career development, interpersonal skills, and human relations programs are often grouped in this section. This is because they have received mixed reviews regarding their overall effectiveness and importance.

No Stars. Programs or activities of this type are perceived as low in relative importance and practical application. They receive little, if any, attention or revenue allocation but will occasionally be offered some. No Star training programs and service activities are used by HRD practitioners to fill the gaps in their training calendar. Motivational training, values clarification, and sensitivity training are examples of this type.

Applying the Portfolio Analysis Model. As we have said elsewhere (Gilley and Eggland, 1989), HRD practitioners can utilize the portfolio analysis model to analyze their training programs and service activities and so determine their importance and applicability. The model can also be used to aid HRD practitioners in the allocation of revenue by identifying training programs and services that will require additional support. By using this model, HRD practitioners can prioritize their training programs and service activities to increase HRD's program effectiveness and efficiency. As a comprehensive approach, the model aids HRD practitioners in time allocation and utilization. Finally, the portfolio analysis model also helps HRD practitioners improve quality by analyzing and organizing training programs and services in a systematic manner that reduces errors and duplication of effort.

What types of strategies can HRD practitioners develop for their programs and service activities?

Once training programs and service activities have been prioritized, one of four fundamental strategies can be applied to each. The strategies can be viewed as a master plan for the HRD program. The four strategies are to build, to hold, to harvest, and to divest (Gilley and Eggland, 1989).

To Build. Many programs and activities require the commitment of additional financial and human resources to reach their full potential. This decision is designed to increase the importance or applicability of a training program or service activity. Programs or activities that have the potential for improving their current position or ranking are subject to this strategy. Therefore, it is very appropriate for strong Wandering Stars and Constant Stars and quite appropriate for Super Stars.

This strategy is the most risky and costly of the four. This is because it requires HRD practitioners to allocate additional resources to improve the position of a training program or service. Failure to improve the perception of the program or service will therefore negatively affect the credibility of the HRD program. Accordingly, HRD practitioners must be convinced of the potential of a program or activity before they select a build strategy. Training programs such as management skills, communication skills, computer skills, and time management programs are ones for which this strategy would be very appropriate (see Figure 6.4).

To Hold. The present financial and human resource allocation of many training programs and service activities is adequate to maintain their present position or rank. This marketing strategy is known as the hold strategy; its primary objective is to maintain a current rank or position of a program or service. It is most appropriate for Super Stars and strong Constant Stars in order to ensure their continued strength. In the case of Wandering Stars, this strategy is only appropriate if the program or service is demonstrating the potential for increased applicability. For other programs or services that have had significant time to demonstrate momentum and have failed to do so, another strategy (to harvest) is more appropriate. Finally, this strategy is appropriate for No Stars that serve to "fill in the gap."

The principal focus of the hold strategy is on long-term results. It is also the most conservative of the four decisions (Gilley and Eggland, 1989). Again, management skills and communication skills programs are candidates for this strategy if the HRD practitioner elects not to enhance their position. All of the programs in the Constant Stars and Wandering Stars categories with the exception of nonverbal communications are candidates for this strategy (Figure 6.4).

To Harvest. Several training programs and service activities have either outlived their usefulness or have never reached their potential. In either case, the continued allocation of financial and human resources to them is not a wise decision. In addition, some programs or services are perceived to have a limited future but fill an important and immediate need. In either case, this strategy is appropriate for short-term results where HRD practitioners desire to maximize the benefits of training programs or service activities. Weak Constant Stars, Wandering Stars with limited potential, and No Stars are best candidates for this strategy. For example, the human relations skills (Constant Stars), nonverbal communications (Wandering Stars), and all of the No Stars programs are candidates for this strategy (Figure 6.4).

To Divest. There is a point in the life of every training program and service activity when the financial and human resources used to support it would be better used to fund another program or service. This strategy involves divesting the resources assigned to one training program or service activity and assigning it to another. It is most common in organizations where training revenue has been cut or limited or when difficult funding decisions must be made. It is also common in organizations where HRD practitioners desire to improve the efficiency of existing training programs or service activities. The divest strategy also gives HRD practitioners a chance to reduce the number of programs and services offered. It is a strategy most often used for weak Wandering Stars that have never developed to their full potential. The No Stars programs that are not being used to fill gaps are candidates for this approach. All of the No Stars programs in Figure 6.4 are ideal for it.

How can HRD practitioners combine the concept life cycle with the portfolio analysis model?

As a training program or service activity moves through the concept life cycle, its portfolio position may also change and with it the strategy. Therefore, HRD practitioners should use the concept life cycle and portfolio analysis in combination to establish which training strategy is most appropriate (Gilley and Eggland, 1989; Gilley, 1987).

Figure 6.5 reflects the various strategies for training programs or services as they move through the life cycle relative to their portfolio position. At any stage of the cycle, a training program or service can be identified in any of four primary positions of the portfolio analysis model. Therefore, the strategy selected will be based upon two factors: the stage the program or service is in, and the position it holds in the model. As these combinations change, different strategies will become more appropriate. For example, the strategy for a training program in the exposure stage and identified as a Super Star would be a build approach. However, if the same Super Star program has entered the maturity stage, the build strategy is not appropriate. In this case, a hold strategy is the first choice and a build strategy the second. The implication of this would be that new financial and/or human resources would not *automatically* be allocated for the further development as well as support of the training program. As this program moved into the decline stage, a hold-harvest strategy would become appropriate, which would mean that the HRD practitioner was positioning it to be phased out or deemphasized. Thus the financial and human resources allocated to maintain this program would begin to be assigned to other, more important and applicable training programs (Gilley and Eggland, 1989; Gilley, 1987).

In addition, a training program or service can change its position in the portfolio analysis as it moves through the concept life cycle. For example, a training program that begins at the ex-

Figure 6.5. Strategies for HRD Programs and Services According to
Their Life Cycle Stage and Importance.

Concept Life Cycle Stage	Importance Applicability Position	Strategy
Exposure	Super Star	Build
	Wandering Star	Hold
	Constant Star	Hold-Harvest
	No Star	No Involvement[a]
Acceptance	Super Star	Build
	Wandering Star	Hold-Build
	Constant Star	Hold-Hold-Build
	No Star	Harvest-Divest
Maturity	Super Star	Hold-Build
	Wandering Star	Hold-Harvest
	Constant Star	Hold-Harvest-Build
	No Star	Harvest-Divest
Decline	Super Star	Hold-Harvest
	Wandering Star	Harvest-Hold
	Constant Star	Divest-Harvest-Hold
	No Star	Divest

[a]During exposure, no involvement means a wait-and-see approach.
Source: Gilley, 1987.

posure stage as a Wandering Star may remain in this category until
the maturity stage, where it becomes a Super Star. As a result of this
change, the practical application of the program will have increased.
Therefore, HRD practitioners will want to reconsider the strategy in
order to reflect the program's present strength. If the training program were to move into the Constant Star category during the decline
stage because its relative importance had declined, a divest-harvest-
hold strategy would appear most appropriate. Figure 6.5 accounts for
many but not all of the possible combinations when the two models
are used together. It should therefore be used as an outline or strategic
planning guide for HRD marketers.

*What type of overall program strategy
should HRD practitioners employ?*

Once HRD practitioners have identified the appropriate life cycle
and portfolio position for each of their training programs or service

activities, they can begin to develop an appropriate overall program strategy. This strategy will indicate the direction in which the HRD program is moving regarding its marketing efforts. In Figure 6.6, four such strategies are identified; practitioners will select one of them according to the configuration of training programs or service activities within their HRD program and the vision they have of the future. The reasoning behind each choice is as follows (Gilley, 1988):

1. Market penetration (top left) calls for increasing the acceptance of a training program or service activity in its current market through more aggressive promotion.
2. Market development (bottom left) consists of offering an existing program or service to a new market segment instead of trying to obtain growth within the current market.
3. A product development strategy (top right) calls for redesigning and developing a "new and improved" version of the program or service that can be reintroduced in existing markets.
4. A diversification strategy (bottom right) is based on the belief that growth can result from offering new training programs or service activities to new markets.

Figure 6.6. Overall Marketing Strategies for HRD Departments.

	Existing Programs	New Programs
Existing Markets	Market Penetration	Product Development
New Markets	Market Development	Diversification

Source: Gilley and Eggland, *Principles of Human Resource Development,* © 1989 by Addison-Wesley Company. Reprinted with permission of the publisher.

Why do training programs and services fail?

The last consideration that HRD practitioners should concern themselves with is the causes of training program or service failure. Peter, Donnelly, and Tarpey (1982) report that they fail for the following reasons:

- Faulty estimates of market potential
- Poor timing in the introduction of a product
- Rapid change in the market (economy) after introduction
- Inadequate control
- Faulty marketing testing
- Inadequate expenditures on initial promotion
- Faulty estimates in production costs
- Improper offerings
- Unexpected reactions from competitors

Each of these must be addressed by HRD marketers in addition to the factors previously discussed.

Conclusion

We identified three different types of HRD products in this chapter: convenience, shopping, and specialty. Each differs in cost, frequency of use, degree of use, and information search time. The type of HRD product offered will greatly affect the marketing strategies developed by HRD practitioners.

Each product was created through the product development process, which consists of five stages: idea generating, idea screening, planning and development, pilot testing, and implementation. Once implemented, training programs and services begin their concept life cycle, a five-stage process consisting of exposure, acceptance, growth, maturity, and decline. The strategies employed to support training programs and services—to build, to hold, to harvest, and to divest—can significantly affect the adoption rate as well as the longevity of a training program or service.

The strategies that HRD professionals employ may depend

upon the relationship between the importance and the applicability of the training program or service. We refer to this comparison as the portfolio analysis, a process that helps determine the type and amount of financial and human resources allocated for each training program or service.

Chapter Seven

Weighing the Costs and Benefits of Proposed Programs

Having developed, shaped, and refined the product in response to the market, the HRD professional will formulate price and location strategies. Effective creation of these strategies is crucial to the marketing success of the HRD department. The program(s) must be offered at the right "price" and in the proper "location" to have any chance for success in the marketplace. Let us see first what price means to an HRD program.

Pricing the HRD Program

Price is one of the most important and complex variables included in the marketing mix. Though used by HRD practitioners in accomplishing the program's goals and objectives, it is often the most misunderstood and abused element in the marketing mix. Many HRD practitioners make the mistake of discounting the importance of price when developing training courses and activities. Since HRD is an internal operation, often no fee is charged for the programs (or the programs are only reimbursed through administrative adjustment in budgets between departments). But certainly, as we saw in Chapter Six, an HRD program is a "product," and each participant is giving up something of value in order to attend a training session. Time, energy, effort, and personal commitment are the most common things that are exchanged for the training received (Gilley and Eggland, 1987).

Price can also be used as an important positioning tool for HRD practitioners. The most important courses and activities should require the most time, energy, effort, and commitment in return for the greater amount of knowledge and skill development. For instance, the HRD practitioners in our insurance company example should analyze and prioritize their training program, determine which of the courses are the most important, and design them according to the principles of the marketing concept.

Price can also be a reflection of the quality of the product. A price that is set too low may suggest a poorly designed and developed training program. A price set too high, on the other hand, may miss the users who perceive the training program as just average and therefore not worth such a price. Indirectly, then, price can determine the success or failure of an HRD program and its survival in the long run.

The Basics of Pricing

To a buyer, price is the value placed on what is exchanged. Something of value—usually purchasing power—is exchanged for satisfaction or utility. Purchasing power depends on a buyer's income, credit, and wealth; but price does not always involve money or some other financial consideration. In fact, trading of products (barter) is the oldest form of exchange.

Buyers' concern for an interest in price is related to their expectations about the satisfaction or utility associated with a product. Since buyers have limited resources, they must allocate their purchasing power. It is they who must decide whether the utility gained in an exchange is worth the purchasing power sacrificed.

Almost anything of value can be assessed by a price because in our society price is the measurement of value commonly used in exchanges. Thus price quantifies value, and is the basis of most market exchanges (Ferrell and Pride, 1982). Indeed, price is probably the most flexible variable in the marketing mix, for marketers usually can adjust their prices more easily and quickly than they can change other marketing mix variables. Even so, under certain circumstances, the price variable may be relatively inflexible. In any case, price is a major concern in completing exchanges between buyers and sellers.

Why is price important?

It can take a great deal of time to develop a product, to plan its promotion, to communicate its benefits to customers, and then to distribute it. Often only price can be changed quickly enough to respond to changes in demand or to the actions of competitors. Price therefore plays a critical role in efficient marketing. Since price often has a psychological impact on customers, marketers can use it symbolically, raising a price to emphasize the quality of a product and increasing the status associated with buying it, or lowering a price to emphasize a bargain and gain thrifty customers. Price can therefore have a strong effect on sales too.

How is pricing done in the HRD realm?

We are accustomed to thinking of price, as the foregoing introduction suggests, in terms of monetary measures. In the area of human resource development, however, prices can take on characteristics in addition to monetary ones. Pricing in the HRD department may include a collection of what are known as *perceived costs*. These may be time spent, risk taken, social capital used, energy expended, resources used, or other costs that may amount to negative outcomes or depletion of resources possessed by the "buyer." When pricing HRD programs, we must consider any and all costs as part of the pricing strategy.

Developing a Pricing Strategy

After the HRD organization has stated its marketing objectives, it can begin to consider an appropriate pricing strategy. Pricing strategies tend to fall into three or four categories. They may be cost oriented, demand oriented, or competition oriented, or reflect some combination of these approaches.

Cost-Oriented Pricing. The practice of cost-oriented pricing refers to setting prices largely on the basis of costs, either marginal costs or total costs, including overhead. Markup pricing is a common form of cost-oriented pricing that is often found in retailing where the merchant adds predetermined but different markups to various goods. Cost-plus pricing, a variation on this theme, is used to describe the pricing of activities that are nonroutine and therefore difficult to "cost" in advance, such as putting on a special training program for a company.

Break-even analysis is the most widely used form of cost-oriented pricing. It is used by many HRD departments to determine how many units of a program would have to be "sold" to fully cover the costs. This is known as the *break-even volume*. To illustrate: the manager of an HRD department wants to set the price for an eight-week program dealing with management development that would cover the total cost of the program. How many managers must be enrolled to do this? To find out, the HRD manager calculates the fixed costs of the program, and the variable costs including food, instructor salaries, and so on. Finally, the manager initially considers charging a $1,000 fee per enrollee. The number of enrollees needed to break even is determined by the intersection of the total revenue and the total cost curve.

Demand-Oriented Pricing. Prices based on the level of demand rather than on costs are known as demand oriented or demand based. The demand-oriented HRD manager would estimate how much value consumers see in the offering and price it accordingly. An executive conference with national recognized speakers, for example, will command a higher price than a program taught by skilled but unknown presenters. The premise of demand-based pricing is that price should reflect the perceived value of the offering in the client's mind. A corollary is that the institution should invest in building up the perceived value of the offering if it wants to charge a higher price. Thus a well-known HRD program supplier that builds a reputation for excellence in programs can charge a higher fee than can an average provider.

Competition-Oriented Pricing. When an HRD organization sets its prices low on the basis of what competitors are charging, its pricing policy can be described as competition oriented. It may choose to charge the same as the competition, a higher price, or a lower price. The distinguishing characteristic is that the organization does not maintain a rigid relationship between its price and its own costs or demand. That is, its cost or demand may change, but it maintains its price position in relation to its competitors. Conversely, the same organization will change its prices when competitors change theirs, even if its own costs or demand have not changed. Since clients often use price as an indicator of quality, an organization may consciously set its fee or price level to establish its position in relation to other organizations.

Setting the Price

There are many approaches to setting prices for services delivered by HRD programs. The model that is presented here is an eclectic one, not to be followed slavishly, but rather to be used as a guide whenever it seems appropriate. It provides a logical way of analyzing the effectiveness of price in the marketing mix and the contributions price makes to an HRD organization's objectives. The model has eight steps in it, as follows:

1. Develop pricing objectives
2. Determine target market's amenability to price and ability to purchase
3. Determine demand
4. Compare demand, cost, and profit
5. Study competitors' prices
6. Select a pricing policy
7. Select a pricing method
8. Select the price

Develop Pricing Objectives. The first step is to develop a pricing objective that fits with the HRD organization's overall objectives and mission. A pricing objective is an overall goal that describes the role of price in an organization's long-range plans. It may be as simple as survival. Most organizations will tolerate short-run losses, internal upheaval, and many other difficulties in their HRD departments if these are necessary conditions for continued existence.

Since price is such a flexible and convenient variable to adjust, it is sometimes used to increase or decrease demand in order to match the company's resources and supplies with fluctuations in other market conditions. Although some private sector businesses sometimes claim that their objective is to maximize profits for their owners, this objective is rarely operational, since it is difficult to measure whether it has been achieved. This is especially true in the nonprofit realm, of course, or in the public sector.

Pricing to attain a specified return on the company's investment is another pricing objective that is related to profit. Many companies set prices using return on investment as an objective, but this goal sometimes has to be altered if the marketing environment changes. Level of market share is selected by some as a pricing objective because a firm's sales in relation to total industry sales is seen as a very meaningful benchmark of success. It is possible, of course, for an organization to increase its market share even though sales for the total industry are decreasing. Finally, some organizations set prices in order to recover cash as fast as possible. These are known as cash-flow objectives. Financial managers watching the human resource development entity understandably are interested in quickly recovering the capital spent to develop products and programs. A disadvantage of this approach could be high prices, which might allow competitors with lower prices to gain a larger share of the market.

Determining the Target Market's Amenability to Price and Ability to Purchase. The clients' attitudes and reactions toward price to some degree determine their acceptance of an HRD program or product. Since price plays a major role in their overall evaluations, it is essential to identify the values that specify their expected transactions as types of buyers. Buyers must need a program, be willing to use their buying power, and have the authority to buy. Their ability to buy, like their evaluation of price, has direct consequences for marketers setting a price. It will do no good if a buyer has a high opinion of the HRD program, but does not possess the ability to purchase.

Determining Demand. The market research activity discussed in Chapter Five is the most important determinant of demand for the

HRD program's output. The techniques that should help to estimate sales potential—the quantity of a service that could be sold
during a specific period of time—are practical approaches to understanding demand.

For most programs there is an inverse relationship between
price and quantity demanded. The quantity demanded goes up as
the price goes down; and as price goes up, quantity demanded goes
down. As long as buyers' needs, ability (purchasing power), willingness, and authority to buy remain stable, and as long as the various
environmental situations remain constant, this fundamental, inverse relationship will continue. Demand can be influenced, however, by changes in buyers' attitude, by other elements in the
marketing mix, and by uncontrollable environmental factors. Although demand fluctuates unpredictably, some HRD organizations
have succeeded in adjusting to such fluctuations by correlating demand for a specific program to demand for the total industry, or to
an economic variable.

Comparing Demand, Cost, and Profit. There are two approaches
to understanding demand, cost, and profit relationships: break-even
analysis and marginal analysis. The point at which the costs of pro-
ducing a program equal the revenue made from selling the program
is the break-even point. If an HRD department has total costs for one
year that amount to $175,000 and in the same year it has charges for
$175,000 worth of programs, then the department has broken even.

The field of economics contributes another useful idea about
costs and pricing: the point of maximum profit is the point at
which the *marginal cost* is equal to the *marginal revenue.* Marginal
revenue is the change in total revenue that occurs after an additional
unit of the program is sold.

Studying Competitors' Prices. In order for an HRD department to
set prices effectively, it must learn competitors' prices. This may be
a regular function of market research. After competitors' prices have
been determined, a company can use price to increase sales.

Selecting a Pricing Policy. A pricing policy is a guiding philosophy
or course of action designed to influence and determine pricing

decisions. Pricing policy provides approaches to achieving pricing objectives for the HRD department, and thus is an important consideration in developing an overall marketing strategy. A general pricing policy should be considered by providing standing answers to the recurring question, How will price be used as a variable in the marketing mix? Pricing policies are guidelines for solving the practical problems of establishing prices. The following are a few examples of pricing policies:

- Price skimming: This approach provides the most flexible introductory base price. Demand tends to be inelastic in the introductory stage of the product life cycle. This means that the price of a product will not have a strong impact on the selection of a specific product or service. Price elasticity refers to the effect incremental changes have upon the adoption or rejection of a product or service. Price skimming permits an organization to charge the highest possible price that buyers who most desire the product will pay.

- Odd-even pricing: This assumption that more of a product will be sold at $999 than at a $1,000 leads to odd-even pricing; supposedly clients will think that the product is a bargain at $999. Also, clients are supposed to think that the organization could have charged $1,000, but instead cut the price to the last cent, to $999 or $995 (which is also an odd price). Some claim, too, that certain types of customers are more attracted by odd prices than by even ones.

- Price leaders: Sometimes a few programs are priced below the usual markup or below cost. The latter are *price leaders;* with their help, management hopes to increase sales of regularly priced merchandise in order to increase total sales volume and profits.

- Superficial discounting: This fictitious comparative pricing, sometimes called "was-is pricing" in the trade, is known as superficial discounting. "Was $1195, now $995" is an example. Legitimate discounts are not questioned, of course, but when pricing policy gives only the illusion of a discount it is unethical and, in some states, illegal.

Selecting a Pricing Method. After selecting a pricing policy, the HRD marketer must choose a pricing method, that is, a mechanical procedure for setting prices on a regular basis. The pricing method structures the calculation and determination of the actual price. The nature of the program, its sales volume, or the number of programs delivered by the organization will determine how prices are calculated. Pricing methods must consider pricing objectives, as well as knowledge about clients, demand, costs, and competition.

Selecting the Price. Finally, pricing policies and methods should direct HRD marketers in selecting a final price. Along the way, an important part of establishing pricing objectives is to learn something about the target market and to determine demand, price elasticity, costs, and competitive factors. The final price will be affected by the role of price in the marketing mix.

Pricing decisions are important to the HRD department, especially its marketing effort, because it normally depends on some form of revenues in order to operate. When practitioners set or change prices, they need to understand how clients perceive price. In addition to monitoring prices, clients are faced with other kinds of "costs." They often use the price as a measure of quality of a service or program. They are particularly interested in the *effective price*—the net amount they must pay—rather than the list price.

HRD organizations planning to change an existing price should take into account how clients and competitors will respond to the price change. Price increases should be announced well in advance and be accompanied by a communications campaign, explaining the reasons for the increase.

Location Strategy for HRD

Applying the concept of location strategy to marketing in HRD runs the risk of being behind the times. In the era when marketing principles were applied only to the distribution of hard and soft goods, the concept of location was simplistic and easily implemented. It involved the channels of distribution through which the manufactured item flowed from the time it left the production facility to the time it was acquired by a consumer, with all of the transportation and storage activities that one would expect to consider when manufacturing and selling a widget. The concept of location or channels of distribution is somewhat more complex, however, in the case of services and even more complex when applied to programs or other offerings of an HRD department. But it is possible and in fact necessary to apply it.

What is an HRD location strategy, and what are the location variables?

A location or distribution strategy involves getting the right programs to the target market at the correct time. A program is not very valuable to a client if it is not available when and where it is wanted and needed.

In the case of HRD programs, location includes the *type of training location:* on the job, in formal classroom settings, off the job, and in independent or self-directed study, as well as the actual *facilities* where the training takes place. Research on adult learning supports the view that a comfortable and supportive environment is conducive to learning and should be considered when training programs are designed and developed, as well as delivered.

Another important location consideration is the *time of day.* Again, users should be consulted before a training program is scheduled. For example, the HRD practitioners in the insurance company example cited earlier might prefer afternoon training sessions; however, their customers—let's say the insurance agents—might prefer early morning training sessions, since afternoons and evenings are their optimal selling period. Failure to adjust to the users' preferred time may establish resistance, which could ultimately affect the outcomes of training as well as the attitudes of employees toward the training program (Gilley and Eggland, 1987).

Another part of the location strategy is the *method of instruction* selected. Several types of training approaches will probably need to be developed, since there is a myriad of human resources to serve the insurance company. In addition, the insurance agents and regional sales managers will most likely be scattered through the state, region, or country, while administrative personnel, underwriters, and corporate executives will be located at the corporate offices. As a result, the HRD practitioners must develop a delivery system that accounts for geographical as well as professional differences.

Another overlooked part of the location strategy is the actual *location of training programs.* All too often, training sessions are scheduled at the training offices or classroom (on the fifth floor of the corporate office building, for instance). While this is convenient for the HRD staff, it might be more convenient, as well as more appropriate, to conduct training in the customer's office or work station. This would save precious minutes of valuable production time. More importantly, it would communicate to the customers that the HRD practitioners respect them and their time. In addition, customers (trainees) are more comfortable in an environment they know—a fact that, if utilized, could become an important advantage to the HRD practitioners.

How can an HRD organization make its programs available and accessible to its target clients?

Availability and accessibility are not the same thing. Suppose an HRD department ran a program to enhance the skills of first-line managers, but the program was located an hour from where most of the managers lived and worked. Suppose further that the program was offered from 9:00 to 12:00 on weekday mornings from September to May, precisely the hours when the managers would be working. We would say that the program, although available, was not accessible to those for whom it was planned. In order to succeed, such a program would have to increase its accessibility, perhaps by offering a location closer to the potential participants and a schedule at a time when the workers were not engaged.

The location and scheduling of programs are critical. Offering a high-quality, appropriately priced program is not enough. Trainees may avoid programs that are in run-down, dangerous urban areas because the surroundings are unpleasant and unsafe. Likewise, they may avoid rural settings that seem isolated and boring. Gone are the days when would-be enrollees put up with long journeys to attend programs with limited offerings, Spartan dormitories, and restrictive rules. In the 1990s, few HRD departments can claim a captive market; clients have many training options. At the same time, there are underserved markets for training programs that can be cultivated.

Some HRD departments, recognizing these market changes, have adopted new schedules, delivery systems, and locations to retain and serve their markets. Realistically, few organizations can make fundamental changes in the short term. They can, however, consider improving their use of existing resources in making training offerings available. Then they can begin planning ways to modify or expand current programs to create more consumer satisfaction.

Trainers usually think first of providing instruction to enrollees. A more complete picture would show a variety of training programs and services, each provided to trainees in a different way. HRD departments often have several different programs, and they need to plan an appropriate location strategy for each one. How these programs and other outputs are made available constitutes the institution's delivery or distribution system. Analyzing the distribution system involves tracing the steps by which the program or service gets directly from the producer to the final consumer, as is the case with most services.

What are the distribution objectives?

In deciding how to distribute its programs and services, the HRD department must consider the nature of each. It must also consider the important characteristics of the consumer, who will ultimately benefit from it. A workable distribution system gets the right product or service to the consumer who wants it, at a cost that both the producer and the consumer can afford. A superior distribution system accomplishes the same task in a way that makes the product easier to obtain and/or reduces the cost for one or both parties.

Planning an effective distribution system involves understanding the consumer, the organization's mission and resources, and the nature of the program or service to be distributed. Consider the major decisions educational institutions often face in designing and operating their distribution systems.

An HRD organization first needs to consider the appropriate distribution objectives. The most basic is what level of convenience should be offered to the enrollees. Obviously, cost will be an issue, but the HRD department might begin by trying to describe the maximum level of service it could offer. For an HRD department the maximum level of service might be to provide individual instruction in each enrollee's home upon request. Few clients would pay for this extra convenience and the supplying institution probably would not be able to afford the cost of providing this level of service to everyone. HRD departments, in fact, must usually offer less than the maximum consumer convenience in order to keep down the costs of distribution. Since virtually all departments have limited resources, they must base their distribution planning on a clear picture of the level and quality of service they will offer.

Should new locations or delivery systems be established?

HRD departments with new or growing markets need to consider whether to offer some of their programs at other locations or through different mediums. Organizations that provide direct services are like retail stores, where people can come in and make their selection and purchase. Like retail businesses, they must decide how many outlets to operate. The most economical decision is to operate a single outlet and have all consumers come to it. This strategy may not, however, result in the largest number of enrollees. An organization may use rented or loaned facilities, convert existing ones, or build new ones. Regardless of the choice, it faces the task of deciding where the new facility should be located. The organization may also consider its desired pattern of distribution. For instructional programs, this step involves deciding whether to have one facility serve everyone, or to establish multiple locations. This decision depends on the enrollee's ability and willingness to travel to facilities. When making this decision, then, the organization must balance the cost of multiple locations with the revenue that will be generated if the multiple locations succeed in attracting more enrollees. These and other questions are central to consideration of whether to establish new facilities or new channels.

The most important factor in facilities planning is how well the facilities will serve the planned training activities. Training departments should also consider the appearance of their facilities, because the atmosphere in which training programs are delivered can affect trainees' attitudes and behavior. Many departments have taken pains to maintain their facilities in a pleasing architectural and design style that makes trainees feel comfortable and at home. No matter what kind of facility is chosen, each will have a look that may add to or detract from consumer satisfaction and employee performance.

Moreover, since HRD practitioners work in the facility all day long, the facility should also be designed to support them in performing their work with ease and cheerfulness. Because of this experience, HRD practitioners are an excellent resource to be used when training facilities are designed.

When should alternative channels or intermediaries be used?

Some training organizations are turning to the telephone, television, radio, computers, and tape recorders to serve their current markets or to attract new ones. The establishment of such electronic classrooms as an alternative requires students and instructors to "meet" at prearranged times and locations. It may therefore be considered too inflexible for many program managers.

Training departments usually produce and then deliver their services directly to their clientele. Yet in many cases, intermediaries are commonly used to assist in the delivery process. In some cases these intermediaries may be able to provide higher quality programs for lower prices because their costs are developed in a different fashion, or because they possess higher levels of expertise, or for a wide variety of additional reasons.

To design an efficient distribution, delivery, or dissemination system, an organization must first decide on what level of convenience it can and should offer to its target market. Often current facilities are poorly matched to the institution's needs. The institution should then consider opening additional facilities and/or using alternative channels to serve its markets. Finally the institution should consider using intermediaries to provide services to assist them in distribution tasks.

Conclusion

Today, HRD professionals must justify the cost of training to organizational leaders. They must also identify the benefits received from training and communicate positive results to others. Selecting an appropriate pricing strategy, therefore, is an important step in establishing a cost/benefit relationship for HRD.

HRD professionals can also demonstrate their value to the organization by offering training programs and services to employees at the right time and place. This form of promoting the marketing concept reflects how far HRD professionals are willing to go in order to provide value to their clients.

Chapter Eight

Raising the Visibility of HRD Within the Organization

Promotion is one of the most important marketing variables that HRD practitioners can use. It involves communication between HRD practitioners and their clients.

The primary purpose of promotion is to improve the image and credibility of HRD. Practitioners should also use promotion to alter perception, beliefs, and attitudes toward HRD. If this is accomplished, the behavior of clients will also be affected, as will be seen from their increased participation in training programs and use of services designed to improve performance and satisfy developmental needs.

A common message should also be shared by HRD practitioners and their clients. This message must include the advantages, benefits, and values of training programs and services. HRD practitioners should use several promotional activities in order to inform, persuade, or remind clients of this message. These activities are commonly referred to as the *promotional mix;* they include *sales promotion* and *personal selling.*

Ferrell and Pride (1982) defined these terms as follows:

Sales promotion is an activity and/or material that acts as an incentive for a client to participate in a training program or use an HRD service.

Personal selling is a process of informing, persuading, and reminding clients to participate in training programs or HRD services through personal communication.

HRD Promotion and the Communication Process

Promotion is a communication process. According to Barker (1981), the communication process is a method of integrating and grouping unrelated "elements" into a whole in order to achieve a desired outcome or goal. In HRD, the outcome or goal is increased participation in training programs and use of HRD services. However, to understand the communication process, you must identify the elements involved and analyze how they affect one another.

What is communication?

There are six elements in the communication process:

1. The source of communication (sender)
2. A message (advantages, benefits, and values)
3. Medium of communication (channel)
4. The receiver of the message (receiver)
5. A return message (feedback)
6. Barriers to communication

We recognize that this model is the familiar classic one of communication, but it still serves to remind us of the process's complexity.

Sender. Here, the senders of promotional communications are the HRD practitioners. They must possess credibility, attractiveness, and power (Barry, 1986). *Credibility* refers to the degree of acceptance clients have for the HRD practitioners. They must be accepted by the executives and upper management that they are trying to influence; otherwise, the message being communicated will not be heard. *Attractiveness* does not refer to physical appearance but to the ability of HRD practitioners to relate to or identify with the audience they are communicating with. Therefore, it is essential that they establish rapport with their potential clients. *Power* refers to the ability of HRD practitioners to control or capture the attention and interest of their clients. Thus HRD practitioners must develop personal presence in order to communicate effectively.

Message. The message refers to what is being communicated. The objective of marketing communications is to inform, persuade, or remind clients to participate in training programs or use HRD services. Therefore, the message must appeal to a performance problem or developmental need of HRD clients or it will go unheeded.

To increase the likelihood of successful communication, HRD practitioners must attempt to construct a message in such a way that clients understand and properly interpret it. Barry suggests that the structure of a message can affect its chances of success. Therefore, how a message is presented will help determine its acceptance.

Channel. In marketing communication, there are two basic types of channels: personal and impersonal. *Personal channels* are face-to-face encounters between HRD practitioners and members of the client group. This group includes participants of training programs and users of HRD services. In addition, centers of influences, who serve as opinion leaders in the organization, are examples of personal channels. They share information through word of mouth to others in the organization.

Impersonal channels include such media as brochures, training calendars, training catalogs, program announcements, and newsletters. HRD practitioners can use these channels to communicate messages when personal appeals are inappropriate. An example would be a large international corporation with offices in over seventy-five cities and fifteen countries. In this situation, it would be impossible to communicate in person with each and every individual interested in training programs and HRD services.

Personal channels are considered more effective while impersonal channels are considered more efficient. In addition, personal channels allow for direct and immediate feedback regarding the message. When an impersonal channel is used it may be impossible to measure, obtain, and/or monitor feedback.

Feedback. This can come in a variety of forms. Feedback can be direct or indirect, verbal or written, solicited or unsolicited, and friendly or unfriendly. It can come from users and nonusers, and/or participants and nonparticipants. Most commonly, two types of feedback exist: impersonal and personal. *Impersonal feedback* is provided by statistics such as the numbers of participants in training programs or users of HRD services. *Personal feedback,* in contrast, is shared during face-to-face conversation with HRD clients.

In most cases, feedback is constructive and genuine and is an expression of a client's point of view and attitude. When negative feedback is expressed it is often because a development need or performance problem was not solved by the training program or service offered by HRD. As a result, HRD practitioners should consider feedback very important, and must incorporate it into the redesign or redevelopment phase of training programs and services.

Barriers to Communication. Barriers to communication are anything that affects or impedes the way a message is received by the HRD client. We have identified five different types:

- Physical barriers
- Cognitive barriers
- Attitudes, beliefs, and values
- Feedback ability
- Noise

In Figure 8.1 we have grouped a number of the most common barriers under the first four types.

Physical Barriers. Physical barriers can be defined as things that interfere with the listener's ability to access stimuli through his or her senses. This means that the listener may not be able to accurately answer the question, What is the message? Barriers of this type can be related to the environment in which the listening is taking place. They can also include the actual physical capacities of the speaker as well as of the listener.

We have identified the following strategies for surmounting each of the physical barriers. All can be used by HRD practitioners to improve promotional communications.

- Try to get away from or stop the distraction.
- Block the distractions out by focusing your attention on what is being said.

Figure 8.1. Barriers to Communication.

PHYSICAL BARRIERS	<ul><li>Noise</li><li>Visual distractions</li><li>Environmental conditions of the interaction</li><li>Volume, rate, and pitch pattern of speaker</li><li>Speaker's vocal quality</li><li>Speaker's appearance</li><li>Listener's hearing ability</li><li>Listener's state of health</li><li>Listener's attentiveness</li></ul>
COGNITIVE BARRIERS	<ul><li>Linguistic overlap (knowledge of the words and/or implications of nonverbal behavior; cultural overlap)</li><li>Familiarity with topic</li><li>Experiential overlap with topic or speaker (quality of experience with speaker or topic; expectations brought to bear)</li><li>Jumping to "meaning" decision without sufficient data</li></ul>
SOCIAL ATTITUDES, BELIEFS, AND VALUES	<ul><li>Knowledge of social rules</li><li>Anticipation of reward/punishment</li><li>Personal bias</li><li>Emotional/logical investment in topic (listener's motivation to listen)</li><li>Personal style</li><li>Anticipated consequences to self-image</li><li>Anticipated effect on status/power</li></ul>
FEEDBACK ABILITY	<ul><li>Ability to give feedback</li><li>Comfort level with topic/speaker</li><li>Personal style</li><li>Desire for information (personal investment in topic/speaker)</li><li>Status/power relationship between speaker and listener (one-up; one-down; one-to-one)</li></ul>

Source: William M. Mercer, Inc. Reprinted with permission.

- Select a seat or position with unobstructed view and free from distractions.
- Assume the role of an efficient listener.
- Listen for concepts and major ideas instead of facts.
- Resist the temptation to stereotype the speaker on the basis of appearance and delivery.

- Be prepared to encounter and respond to different types of speakers.
- Be determined to exert yourself, both physically and mentally, during the listening event.
- Direct attention to and sustain concentration on the speaker and the message throughout the interaction.
- Plan well and in advance for lengthy periods of listening.

Cognitive Barriers. These are barriers that limit the listener's ability to comprehend the meaning of the message. The most common are

- Linguistic overlap: The degree of similarity between the speaker's and listener's language and culture
- Experiential overlap: The common experiences that the listener and speaker have
- Familiarity: The degree of familiarity that the listener has with the topic

Each of these barriers can cause the message to be misunderstood. For example, the language used in a newsletter or brochure, if it is not understood by the client, could be considered a barrier to the communication process.

HRD practitioners must create a fourfold personal professional development plan to overcome these barriers.

1. They should participate in activities and seminars that will broaden the scope of their knowledge. This would be very important for new HRD practitioners entering an unfamiliar industry.
2. They should prepare in advance for difficult topics by reading or inquiring about them. This will help them improve their concentration and comprehension. In turn, communications will improve.
3. They must learn to listen to the entire message of a client before drawing a conclusion. This require concentration and the util-

ization of active listening skills. We will be examining active listening in more detail in Chapter 9.

4. They should increase their vocabulary and broaden their work and life experiences as a way of overcoming this barrier to communications. Additional study of human behavior and development will also provide insight and improve communications.

Social Attitude, Value, and Belief Barriers. These all act to limit an HRD practitioner's ability to respond to a message. Social rules dictate what is permissible, what will be rewarded, and what will be punished. In order to better manage their responses, effective HRD practitioners must become aware of the limitations and potential biases inherent in the attitudes, values, and beliefs they hold.

In order to overcome barriers of this type, we would recommend the following strategies:

- Develop specific methods of controlling your emotions while listening.
- Listen to the client's entire message before judging and refuting.
- Identify your motive for listening.
- Take complete and comprehensive notes.

Feedback Barriers. It is very important to grasp that the communication process is not a linear one, but is interactional. Messages do not "flow" through the system; individuals engage in a process of mutual and simultaneous stimulation. The responsibility for effective communication belongs to both the HRD practitioner and the client.

Our ability to understand a client's message is limited by our ability and willingness to give or receive feedback about that message. Specific barriers can be described as follows:

1. *Ability to give feedback:* An HRD practitioner will be either more or less likely to give feedback to the client depending on his or her skill at doing so. Familiarity with both verbal and nonverbal methods of giving feedback increases the likelihood that messages will get clarified quickly and miscommunication will be avoided.

2. *Comfort level with topic/client:* We may hesitate to engage in the give-and-take of feedback if we are not comfortable with the topic or the client. We may feel out of our depth in the topic area and, for fear of looking stupid, hesitate to ask questions that could clarify the message. Thus anticipating a negative response on the part of the client, we hesitate to engage in conflict.

3. *Personal style:* As with attitudes, values, and beliefs, our personalities will have an effect on our willingness to give or take feedback. For example, an introvert will be much less likely to risk the interpersonal contact of feedback than an extrovert.

4. *Desire for information:* Our need for clarity, as well as the importance of the message, will effect our willingness to overcome other barriers such as discomfort with the client or personal style.

5. *Status/power relationship between HRD practitioner and client:* Most interpersonal relationships can be described in power terms as being "one-up," "one-down," or "one-to-one." We are much more likely to give feedback in a one-to-one or a one-down relationship than we are to give feedback to clients we perceive as being of higher power or status.

HRD practitioners can improve their feedback skills by employing the following strategies:

- Do not fake attention or pretend to listen. Clients can usually identify a fake attention act.
- Respond and transmit meaningful nonverbal cues: maintain good eye contact, hold an attentive body posture, use appropriate facial expressions, and allow gaps of silence in order to provide clients the opportunity to express themselves.
- Actively employ verbal response techniques to improve comprehension. These include clarifying, encouraging, and tentative analysis (see Figure 9.1).

Noise. Noise can be defined as any auditory distraction that prevents or interferes with the sending of a message. For example, a loud conversation in the next office, which disrupts the conversation between a manager interested in an employee training program and an HRD practitioner, is an example of physical noise. A less apparent type of noise could be demonstrated by the effects of an HRD client's lack of interest in the message communicated by an HRD practitioner. This could cause a lack of understanding regarding the purpose of a training program or its intended outcomes. In addition, the lack of credibility, attractiveness, and/or power on the part of an HRD practitioner, as well as the inappropriate use of a communication channel, can create noise in this sense.

Noise must be accounted for by HRD practitioners and adjustment made accordingly. HRD marketers must also be aware of this communication variable, which can affect senders, messages, channels, receivers, and feedback. They should not develop promotion strategies until the sources of noise have been identified, isolated, and adjusted to. In addition, these variables should be viewed as a quality assurance check for HRD marketers before they implement promotional activities.

What are the purposes of promotion?

Sales promotion and personal selling maintain a common set of purposes: to inform, persuade, or remind clients of the advantages, benefits, and values of training programs and services. Each of these purposes will be addressed in detail in this section.

To Inform. As we stated earlier, promotion is a communication process. Therefore, HRD practitioners must communicate the message they want clients to hear. This is often a simple message regarding the purpose and intent of HRD. The message can also include making them aware of the training programs and services that are available. Another informative activity includes identifying the HRD practitioners and their respective areas of expertise. Each of these activities is for the express purpose of informing clients about the HRD program, its programs, its services, and its practitioners.

To Persuade. Another purpose of promotion is to persuade potential clients to participate in training programs or use HRD services. Promotion may be as simple as recommending a particular training program to supervisors in order to improve their employees' performance. Whatever the promotional activity is, if it is effective, clients will take action. In order to accomplish this purpose, the message must be persuasive. If it is to be persuasive, it should appeal to one or more of the developmental needs or performance problems of HRD clients (Warmke and Palmer, 1985).

To Remind. Some messages are sent simply to remind potential clients of the training programs and/or services that are available. This approach becomes important when a training program or service has reached the maturity stage of the concept life cycle (see Chapter Six), and can often be forgotten by clients as they consider newer programs and services. It is important to remember that, as we saw in Chapter Three, many HRD clients do not choose to participate in training programs or use services until very late in the adoption process. Therefore, it is essential that HRD practitioners continue to remind clients of their availability.

What is the AIDA model and how can it be used by HRD practitioners?

In order to maximize the effectiveness of their promotional strategy, HRD practitioners must develop communication messages that produce the desired results. An important part of this activity is identification of clients' responsiveness to the messages they receive. Four categories of response can be identified: attention, interest, desire, and action. Together, these responses form the AIDA model. People's responses to promotional stimuli are a variable combination of knowledge (cognitive), attitudes and feelings (affective), and reactions (conative), according to the model (McCarthy and Perreault, 1984).

Promotional activities must first be designed to gain HRD clients' *attention*. Once the clients are aware of the training programs and services that are available, promotional activities must then arouse their *interest*. This can be accomplished best by communicating the advantages, benefits, and values of training programs and services. Promotional activities must reveal how a particular program or service can solve clients' problems and meet their needs. If successful, the promotional activity should produce a *desire* to participate in training programs or use HRD services. HRD clients will then take *action* based upon their desire to solve their performance deficiencies or satisfy developmental needs.

HRD practitioners can develop promotional activities that gain attention, arouse interest, create desire, or promote action. In this way, promotional activities can be tailored to circumstances within the organization. For example, an HRD practitioner in a new HRD program may wish to introduce the training programs that are available to the organization's employees. She or he would develop promotional activities to gain the attention of potential clients. In other situations, HRD practitioners might need to develop an entirely different type of promotional activity.

What is the relationship between the purposes of promotion, the adoption process, and the AIDA model?

A relationship between the purpose of promotion (to inform, persuade, remind), the adoption process (awareness, interest, evaluation, trial adoption) and the AIDA model (attention, interest, desire, action) can be seen in Figure 8.2. Each of these has been further classified into the three primary orientations of promotional activity that are designed to affect other people's knowledge (cognitive), attitudes (affective), and behaviors (conative). The figure reveals the similarities between the adoption process and the AIDA model, and

Figure 8.2. Relationship Between AIDA Model, Adoption Process, and Purpose of Communication.

Orientation	AIDA Model	Adoption Process	Purpose of Promotion
Cognitive (knowledge)	Attention	Awareness	To Inform
Affective (attitudes)	Interest	Interest	To Persuade
	Desire	Evaluation	
Conative (behavior)	Action	Trial	To Remind
		Adoption	

can help HRD practitioners develop appropriate promotional activities to accomplish the desired purpose. At the same time, HRD practitioners can design promotional activities to improve HRD clients' knowledge, attitudes, and behaviors regarding HRD. Regardless of which approach HRD practitioners choose, the purposes of promotion can be accomplished.

Let us provide an illustrative example. If an HRD practitioner's promotion objective is to persuade clients to increase their participation in training programs, his or her promotional activities would have to be focused on creating a "desire" for them. Therefore, the promotional effort would be directed at changing the attitudes and feelings (affective orientation) that clients have toward training programs and services offered by the HRD program. Thus a message would be created to help stimulate interest in training programs and services. Once this was accomplished, the HRD practitioner would concentrate on encouraging this group to participate in a training program or use an HRD service on a temporary basis (evaluation and trial). If the training program and/or service helped the client satisfy a developmental need or improve performance, satisfaction would result. This would affect the clients' attitudes and feelings toward participating in future training programs and/ or using additional HRD services in the future. As a result, the purpose of the promotion would be accomplished.

What are the factors affecting the selection of promotional activities?

Several factors will affect selection of the particular promotional activity used by HRD practitioners. The most important ones are the nature of the programs, activities, products, or services offered; the marketing objectives of the HRD program; the product strategy identified; and the HRD budget.

Nature of Training Programs and Services. Typically, HRD practitioners rely on program announcements or catalogs for their promotional effort. At the same time, many of them wonder why more people do not participate in training programs or use services. The reason is simple. Most of the training and the services are too complex to communicate effectively through a simple program announcement or catalog. In addition, program announcements and catalogs are most effective as promotional activities that inform or remind HRD clients of training programs and services. If HRD practitioners desire to improve participation in their programs or use of their services, personal selling is required. This is because personal selling is a more personalized and persuasive promotional activity.

It follows that the nature of training programs and services will have a great impact on the kind of promotional activity selected. For example, a team building program is very complex and involved. Therefore, it would require a promotional activity that allowed HRD practitioners the opportunity to explain the purpose and benefits of the program to their clients. In this situation, the most appropriate promotional activity would be personal selling, because it would allow the practitioners to discuss the details of the program and answer questions regarding its purposes, benefits, values, and applications. Another promotional activity could include sales promotions that would emphasize the values and outcomes of team building. This will serve as a reminder of the information shared by HRD practitioners during personal selling activities.

Marketing Objectives of the HRD Program. Before a promotional activity is selected, the marketing objectives of the HRD program must also be considered. If their primary objective is to enhance the HRD program's image, sales promotion would be an effective promotional activity. If, however, the objective is to increase participation in training programs, personal selling would be a much more effective technique. But if the objective is to improve the awareness of clients about upcoming training programs or possible services, program announcements and brochures would be most appropriate. Remember, the promotional activity selected should be directly related to the marketing objectives identified.

Program Strategy. In Chapter Six we introduced the concept life cycle and portfolio analysis. These models enable HRD practitioners to develop an appropriate program strategy for training programs or services offered by the HRD program. Any promotional activity selected should be based on the program strategy identified. This will help HRD practitioners allocate financial and human resources for training programs or services that are perceived to have growth potential and/or are viewed as essential to the organization. In addition, the program strategy takes into account the performance deficiencies and developmental needs of HRD clients. Therefore, the training programs and services designed to address these problems and needs should be promoted more aggressively than those not considered essential.

The HRD Budget. The size of the HRD budget will greatly affect the promotional activities selected. Some promotional activities are much more expensive than others. For example, it is more expensive to reach potential participants for a training program through personal selling than through catalogs and brochures. The promotional activities selected must be within the budget of the HRD program.

Sales Promotion

Sales promotion is a very important part of the promotional strategy. HRD practitioners use it primarily to make clients aware of training programs or services. But several other objectives of sales promotion activities can be identified. They include

- To encourage greater participation in training programs and greater usage of services
- To educate HRD clients about improvements in training programs or services
- To stabilize a fluctuating demand state

Once the objectives have been identified, it is important to review sales promotion techniques that are appropriate for HRD.

How can HRD practitioners use sales promotion to improve the credibility and image of HRD?

The techniques available for HRD promotion include point-of-purchase material, calendars and catalogs, newsletters and program announcements, and brochures.

Point-of-Purchase Material. The materials of this type used by HRD practitioners consist primarily of logos and standardized colors. These are used on binders, letterhead, program announcements, catalogs, and brochures. Their purpose is to draw attention to the HRD program indirectly. Point-of-purchase materials also serve to remind HRD clients of the program.

Let us provide an example of the effectiveness of this type of sales promotion material. The HRD program at the Arthur Andersen Corporation has developed a professional logo that is used on all of its training materials. At their Corporate Learning Center in St. Charles, Illinois, several hundred training and education programs involving more than fifteen thousand of their employees are conducted each year. On the third floor of their classroom building over fifty training programs, in colorful binders, are on display in the Partners Conference Room. Each of these programs represents hundreds of hours of research and development. Each program binder maintains the HRD programs logo, with consistent colors and typeface. Anyone attending a meeting in this room will be impressed with this display. The ultimate beneficiary is the HRD program and its practitioners because such a display communicates the depth and breadth of the HRD program—its quality and the importance of HRD to the organization.

Figure 8.3 provides an example of the logos used by the HRD program at William M. Mercer. These logos are used on letterhead, training program binders, program announcements, catalogs, and training materials. The HRD program also uses consistent colors in order to reinforce its image.

Calendars and Catalogs. Many HRD programs issue calendars and catalogs. Their primary function is to inform clients of upcoming training programs. Calendars are also used as a promotional tool to remind HRD clients of the training programs and services available. In other words, calendars keep the name of the HRD program in front of potential HRD clients. The Education and Training Department of the Technical Center of ALCOA publishes quarterly training calendars and distributes them to managers, supervisors, and engineers. This is done to help employees plan their future

Figure 8.3. Corporate Logos for William M. Mercer, Inc.

PROFESSIONAL
DEVELOPMENT

| Professional Development | New York Region |

CENTRAL REGION

training and education activities as well as to promote the HRD program.

Catalogs are another favored form of sales promotion for HRD programs. A catalog is a list of available training programs and services with complete descriptions and specifications. Its primary purpose is to inform and remind HRD clients of future training activities. But it can also serve as a way of communicating the depth and breadth of the HRD program, and so improve the credibility of HRD. In addition, a catalog provides an HRD program with the opportunity to promote several training programs and services to clients at one time. It is therefore the most cost-effective promotional activity HRD practitioners can use.

Newsletters and Program Announcements. Many HRD programs communicate with their clients through a newsletter. The purpose of this promotional technique is to inform users about the program and its services. It is an excellent way to introduce clients to the HRD practitioners within the organization. For instance, newsletters can include information about a recent training session and who attended it, or they can announce upcoming programs and services. Changes in training time or location as well as other important information can also be given. In addition, newsletters can be used as vehicles for introducing new ideas regarding supervision or management. Several HRD programs use newsletters to communicate with essential clients. Among them are ALCOA's Education and Training Department, General Dynamics's Engineering Training and Development Department, and the Human Resource Development department of William M. Mercer, Inc.

Program announcements are another promotional activity used by HRD programs. They are short, usually one page or less, and contain pertinent messages, to inform or remind clients to participate in upcoming training programs or utilize HRD services. Because they are inexpensive, they can and should be used on an ongoing basis to fill the gap between copies of the newsletter or catalog. They are strictly promotional pieces, while newsletters and catalogs are viewed more as educational mediums.

Brochures. The favored form of sales promotion is the brochure. Its purpose is to communicate in detail the advantages, benefits, and values of training programs and services. Brochures come in every shape and size. They are designed to provoke a client into taking action, that is, participate in training programs or use HRD services. The other sales promotion activities are designed only to inform or remind HRD clients. Brochures, however, should be designed and developed in the same manner as other persuasive mediums. According to Ferrell and Pride (1982) this includes six steps:

1.   To identify a developmental need or performance problem
2.   To suggest that the training programs or services being promoted are the best way to satisfy the identified need or solve the problem
3.   To identify the advantages, benefits, and values of training programs or services
4.   To identify why programs and services are the best ones for the client
5.   To substantiate claims and advantages
6.   To ask the client to take action.

A word of caution: brochures are many times overused as a promotional activity. They may have limited impact and will not be effective in all situations. Therefore, other promotional activities should be incorporated into the promotional strategy as well.

   Sales promotions are best when used along with other parts of the promotional strategy. They serve primarily to inform and remind clients of training programs they should participate in and services they should use.

Conclusion

The right promotional strategy is very important to the successful enhancement of HRD. Practitioners must understand the components and elements of the communications process in order to effectively develop appropriate promotional activities. In addition, they must focus all promotional activities on one of three purposes: to inform, to persuade, and to remind clients of the training programs and services available. They must also utilize the information provided from the adoption process and the AIDA model to correctly develop an optimal orientation for promotional activities. Finally, the factors that affect the selection of these activities must be identified.

HRD practitioners can utilize sales promotion to accomplish several different objectives. The type of sales promotional activities selected will depend upon the marketing objectives identified. Once these have been identified, several sales promotion techniques can be used. They include point-of-purchase materials, program announcements, calendars, catalogs, and brochures.

Chapter Nine

Communicating the Values and Benefits of HRD Persuasively

"Everybody lives by selling something," Robert Louis Stevenson once said. This includes HRD practitioners responsible for training programs and services. However, most HRD practitioners are not willing to admit their responsibility for this activity. Perhaps the reason for such resistance is the negative connotations of the term "selling" or the image salespersons manifest.

Dimensions of Client Resistance

Personal selling is very much needed to improve the image of HRD and its credibility within organizations. It is also an essential activity for promoting the advantages, benefits, and values of training programs and services. HRD practitioners must master the art of selling if HRD is ever to be perceived as an essential component of the organization. It is a promotional activity that cannot be overlooked or ignored by HRD practitioners.

What concerns do HRD clients have about selling and the selling process?

HRD practitioners must realize that clients maintain four attitudes toward selling and the selling process. They are (1) no trust, (2) no need, (3) no help, and (4) no support. Let us examine each of these in detail.

172

Attitude 1: No Trust. Many times, HRD practitioners enter into a selling situation with clients with little or no history of involvement with them. Clients are often skeptical of the practitioners' motives and/or even distrusting of the recommendations they provide. This attitude could be the result of a bad experience with HRD. In any case, it is an attitude that must be overcome.

We believe that the reason for such behavior is that no trust exists between the HRD practitioner and the client. An open and honest discussion about the performance problems and developmental needs of the client will not occur until a trusting relationship has been established between the two. Accordingly, this becomes the first phase in the selling process: *developing rapport with clients.*

Attitude 2: No Need. Another attitude that clients have toward selling and the selling process is that of "no need." This is brought about by HRD practitioners' failure to examine the clients' situation before recommending a solution. Thus the practitioners' recommendations are not being viewed by the clients as credible. HRD practitioners must therefore analyze their clients' situation thoroughly before making a recommendation. This, then, becomes the second phase of the selling process: *discovering performance and developmental needs of clients.*

Attitude 3: No Help. A third attitude common among HRD clients is known as "no help." Under this condition, the clients are skeptical of the solutions being recommended by HRD practitioners. They view the answer to their problems and needs differently from the practitioners. This condition often exists because practitioners do not base their recommendations on the identified performance problems and developmental needs discovered during the second phase of the selling process. An even more serious problem is that many HRD practitioners avoid this phase altogether. As a result, they have nothing to base their recommendations on other than lucky guessing. Therefore, they are no help to the client. This becomes the focus of the third phase of the selling process: *presenting solutions to clients.*

Attitude 4: No Support. Many training programs are provided as a single solution to very complex problems. In addition, many are not designed to improve performance or satisfy developmental needs. HRD practitioners also fail to develop follow-up activities and exercises that reinforce behavioral change and skill acquisition. All of these factors combine to produce the fourth attitude of HRD clients: no support.

HRD practitioners must understand that clients participate in training programs and use HRD services in order to solve performance problems and satisfy developmental needs. Therefore, dissatisfaction with an HRD solution will create bad feelings toward the HRD program and its practitioners. This causes the "no trust" attitude to resurface and so hurts HRD within the organization. As a result, HRD practitioners must be very supportive of clients' decisions and satisfy unhappy clients. This is the fourth phase of the selling process: *supporting clients' decisions and conclusions.*

HRD Practitioner Attitude:
The Problem-Solving Approach

HRD practitioners who focus their attention on improving performance problems and satisfying developmental needs are considered responsive. They have adopted the marketing concept as their philosophy. In order for this to occur HRD practitioners must be as concerned for their clients' improvement as they are with advancing the well-being of HRD. This attitude is known as the "problem-solving approach." With it the HRD practitioners and their clients work collaboratively toward the selection of appropriate training programs and services.

In order to address the client's four attitudes toward selling, HRD practitioners must adopt the problem-solving approach. This approach has four phases. As we have just seen, they are (1) developing rapport with clients; (2) discovering performance problems and/or developmental needs; (3) presenting solutions to clients; (4) supporting clients' decisions and conclusions. Each will now be examined in detail.

Phase 1: Developing Rapport with Clients

Rapport is defined as an open, honest relationship between the client and the HRD practitioner. This condition is not a superficial relationship but is based on a deep concern for the well-being of clients. It is established through the HRD practitioner's sincere interest in and acceptance of the client.

The result of developing rapport is the creation of a definitive working relationship that enhances communication between the client and the HRD practitioner. It can be observed in HRD practitioners who are equally concerned for the relationship they have with the client and for the well-being of HRD.

One of the most difficult processes for HRD practitioners to master is to become participatory, since it requires them to have the courage to relinquish control and dominance over their clients. The participatory approach requires a gentle shift from authoritarian control to participation. In this way it is less threatening to clients. Participation also allows clients to become active agents, which helps them support the decisions made.

The participatory approach requires HRD practitioners to recognize the importance of having a functional working relationship with clients. Practitioners must recognize that clients bring a great deal of experience to a situation, and that this is an invaluable asset to be acknowledged, tapped, and used. However, many practitioners fail to recognize that this asset can provide a wealth of information that would be beneficial in a working relationship. Such recognition is indeed difficult but is essential in the development of positive rapport.

The first step in the development of a participatory approach is to create an environment where a free exchange of ideas and feeling is encouraged. The benefit of this type of environment is that clients feel secure. Clients will also recognize that the lines of two-way communication are open. However, a sharing environment goes beyond the superficial to demonstrate a deep concern for the well-being of clients. It is dedicated to the improvement of performance and satisfaction of developmental needs.

A closer examination reveals that certain key elements are needed for the proper sharing environment to be developed. These ingredients are essential to the success of HRD practitioners. They include acceptance, attentiveness, empathy, genuineness, involvement, understanding, and credibility.

Acceptance. Acceptance is the basic attitude an HRD practitioner holds toward a client. It requires respect for the client as a person of worth. HRD practitioners can demonstrate acceptance by being willing to allow clients to differ from one another. This willingness is based on the belief that each client is a complex being made up of different experiences, values, and attitudes. As Carl Rogers (1961) stated in his classic work *On Becoming a Person,* "by acceptance I mean a warm regard for him/her as a person of unconditional self-worth . . . an acceptance of and a regard for his/her attitudes . . . no matter how negative or positive."

Attentiveness. This refers to the effort made by HRD practitioners to hear the message conveyed by clients. It requires skills in listening and observing. Too many HRD practitioners cannot wait until a client stops speaking so that they can present their own point of view. This diminishes the importance of the client's ideas and communicates a lack of respect for the client. On the other hand, listening conveys to clients that the HRD practitioners are interested in and sensitive to their feeling and thoughts.

Nonverbal communication is also important in establishing and maintaining an environment that is conducive to sharing. Many clients are quite aware of the nonverbal behavior of HRD practitioners and often avoid certain topics and discussions as a result. In fact, this might even lead a client to avoid contact with a particular HRD practitioner. A simple nonverbal technique such as proper eye contact can greatly improve the communication between a client and an HRD practitioner.

Empathy. Typically, empathy has been described as putting oneself in the other person's shoes—attempting, in other words, to see things from another person's vantage point. HRD practitioners who have the ability to feel and describe the thoughts and feelings of others can be considered empathetic. Empathetic understanding is the ability to recognize, to sense, and to understand the feelings that another person communicates through his or her behavioral and verbal expressions, and to accurately communicate this understanding to that person. It is not enough for HRD practitioners to understand the behavior or feelings of clients; they must also communicate that understanding to them. This will help empathy become an active event rather than a passive one.

Genuineness. This refers to the HRD practitioners' ability to be themselves in all situations rather than playing a part or role. Genuineness is demonstrated when HRD practitioners know their true feelings and act on them, as well as being able to communicate them if necessary. Genuineness implies being honest and candid with oneself while functioning as a HRD practitioner, and not pretending to be something one is not. This also implies self-disclosure, but does not mean that one should totally unveil one's personal and private life. Clients want to believe in their HRD practitioners. Honesty and candor provide the atmosphere for this to take place.

Involvement. A willingness to care and feel responsible for the other person is rightly called involvement. While acceptance and understanding are passive, involvement implies action; it means active participation in the client's problems and needs. Only active HRD practitioners can become agents for change. This implies that practitioners should engage in activities that allow face-to-face contact with clients. Maintaining good records of interactions and training activities will demonstrate the interest that the practitioners have in their clients.

Understanding. What we mean by understanding is recognizing and correctly interpreting the feeling, thinking, and behavior of another person. While we acknowledge that no HRD practitioners fully understand their clients, it can be said that understanding clients is essentially a process of sharing. In other words, clients express themselves through verbal and nonverbal language and HRD practitioners attempt to interrupt their meaning and put it into words in order to clarify it for both of them. Understanding can be characterized as external or internal. *External understanding* refers to an awareness of clients' behavior and actions on the part of

HRD practitioners. This means being able to identify the actions of clients and account for the results. *Internal understanding* refers to the ability of HRD practitioners to step into the perceptual world of clients. This is done in an effort to discover their internal world—their fears, successes, and failures. It is at this level that genuine communication can begin.

Credibility. In order to develop credibility HRD practitioners should combine four approaches:

1. *Attempt to identify with clients.* This includes identifying with their interests and expectations. It can also include business customs and behavior. Dress and manners are other areas with which HRD practitioners must identify. One of the most important areas of concern should be speech and language. HRD practitioners must be willing to communicate with clients at their level. Many times we use terminology that clients cannot relate to. This is one of the fastest ways of destroying a relationship with a client. In addition, HRD practitioners must communicate using terms that clients value. Return on investment, profitability, operational results, cost-effectiveness, improved efficiency, quality performance, revenue enhancement—these are simple terms, but they can help HRD practitioners demonstrate their awareness of organizational issues.

2. *Develop mutual interest with clients.* Establishing mutual interest may require self-disclosure. HRD practitioners can also use open-ended questions that search out and highlight common history, ideas, and experiences. Using third-party references is also an excellent way to identify mutual interest. This technique is used to identify a common experience or mutual acquaintance. The process is not one designed to trick clients or develop a superficial relationship with them; it should be a genuine attempt to develop commonality.

3. *Communicate the purpose of the meeting.* In this way, HRD practitioners can share their motives with clients. This helps the clients determine if the HRD practitioner has a true problem-solving purpose. Clients can then judge if the development of a relationship can be beneficial.

4. *Demonstrate professional competence.* This refers to the

HRD practitioners' ability to solve clients' problems and meet their needs. Practitioners can do this without bragging. If they can communicate properly, HRD practitioners should share information about their background, education, training, skills, and track record. They should also communicate their knowledge of the client's situation and the performance problems and developmental needs that other clients in similar situations are facing.

What procedure should HRD practitioners follow during the early part of each meeting with clients?

When meeting with a client, HRD practitioners can use a procedure that communicates their purpose. We refer to it as *goal/agenda/benefit* (GAB). This procedure communicates your empathy for the client, and your appreciation for the client's problems and needs. GAB should help clients gain confidence in you as a person who wants to help them.

GAB statements describe

- Why you are there
- How you would like to proceed
- The potential benefit to them for spending time with you

Goal Statements. These let the client know the specific reason or objective for your meeting. They answer the question, Why are you here? An example would be: "My goal today is to share some information about myself, my colleagues in HRD, our program, and the training programs and services we offer. I would also like to find out more about you and your department's problems and needs. Is that agreeable with you?"

Agenda Statements. These tell the client what you are going to do and suggest a procedure or way to do it. They answer the question, How will we proceed? Disclosing the agenda you intend to follow reduces tension because it helps the client know what to expect. It also reinforces your problem-solving purpose because it describes the steps you will follow toward a goal. An example would be: "I would like to begin by discussing the professional background of my colleagues and myself. Next, I would like to overview the eleven training programs we offer and explain their purposes. Finally, I would like to get to know you better, and obtain a better understanding of your situation, your people, and their professional development needs."

Benefit Statements. These tell the client how the meeting will benefit both you and the client. They answer the question, How will we both benefit from spending time together? You might say, for example: "We hope you will learn something about us, we'll learn something about you, and together we'll determine whether or not our group is a potential resource for meeting your department's performance problems and developmental needs."

What techniques are required for HRD practitioners to develop long-lasting interpersonal relationships with clients?

We believe that establishing a rapport with clients plus using the GAB statements will lead to more successful client meetings. We have also identified ten communication techniques that play a critical role in relating successfully with clients. Figure 9.1 outlines the techniques and links them to the goals that are typically sought through the communication process. Each technique can be learned by virtually any HRD practitioner and is helpful in guiding the exchange process.

Active Listening. One of the agreed-upon keys to effective communications is to become a better listener. Good listening is an important bridge to understanding because it changes the entire relationship between HRD practitioner and client. Some 70 to 80 percent of our waking hours are spent in communication and over half of that time involves listening. Feedback is also a necessary ingredient in effective communication and one that can be made accurate only through good listening.

The difference between active and inactive listening is the difference between listening and just hearing. The act of listening requires effort and concentration. Listening to clients intently can help an HRD practitioner more readily capture the content and

Figure 9.1. Techniques and Goals for Interpersonal Communication.

	Technique	*Goal*
1.	ACTIVE LISTENING	Hearing and clearly understanding what is being said, by concentrated involvement in the communication process with the employee
2.	CLARIFYING	Getting employee elaboration on feelings or attitudes to benefit understanding
3.	ENCOURAGING	Supportive statements or gestures that let the employee know that the supervisor can accept or empathize with his or her approach
4.	INTERPRETING	Dealing with cause-and-effect relationships, apparent from the supervisor's own knowledge and the worker's comments, to understand the implications
5.	PARAPHRASING	Demonstrating an understanding of a worker's ideas by restating them in your words
6.	QUESTIONING	Using inquiry to help pull together the interaction
7.	SILENCE	Intentional pauses that help adjust the pace of interaction
8.	SUMMARIZING	Tentative overall conclusion of what has transpired in the interaction, to check levels of agreement and understanding by the participants
9.	REFLECTING	Mirroring the subordinate's message content with an estimate stating what his/her feelings and attitudes are believed to be
10.	TENTATIVE ANALYSIS	Partial conclusion based on initial public testing of one idea expressed by the worker

Source: Gilley and Moore, 1986, p. 52. Reprinted with permission from HRMagazine (formerly Personnel Administrator), published by the Society for Human Resource Management, Alexandria, Va.

intended meaning. Moreover, since HRD practitioners also convey respect through active listening, certain positive results can be predicted. That is, clients who are listened to attentively will tend to

- Consider their point of view to be more important
- State their feelings and thinking more clearly

- Listen to others more carefully when they speak
- Become less quarrelsome
- Become more receptive to different points of view

In order to develop better listening skills, HRD practitioners should

1. Concentrate all their physical and mental energies on listening
2. When possible, avoid interrupting the speaker
3. Demonstrate interest and alertness
4. Seek an area of agreement with the client
5. Search for meaning and avoid getting hung up on specific words
6. Demonstrate patience (Remember, you can "listen faster" than the client can speak)
7. Provide clear and ambiguous feedback to the client
8. Repress the tendency to respond emotionally to what is said
9. Ask questions when you do not understand something
10. Withhold evaluation of the message until the client is finished and you are sure you understand the message

Clarifying. The HRD practitioner makes clarifying statements in an attempt to place the client's feeling and attitudes in a clear and more recognizable form. The practitioner may also ask the client to elaborate on a particular point or statement in order that the meaning can be more clearly understood. To this end, the client may be asked to provide an example or illustration. It is important to remember that this technique should not be used in a direct effort to interpret the client's feelings or identify the cause of her or his problem; it should be used here only to "test" understanding. A practitioner using this technique would ask questions such as, "Are you angry at not being selected to participate in the team-building workshop?"

Encouraging. This technique enables HRD practitioners to continue elaborating on their feeling and thoughts. Supportive remarks by HRD practitioners such as "I understand," "It's OK to feel that way," "That's interesting, tell me more," or "I hear you," are useful in countering feelings of inadequacy on the part of clients. They also prompt action by encouraging the client to continue the discussion. Another effective technique is a nod of the head or an "mm-hm." They can serve to strengthen the client's response and his or her efforts to continue speaking. This technique lets the client know you are listening but does not interrupt.

Interpreting. When using this technique, HRD practitioners go beyond the client's statement to explain cause-and-effect relationships and clarify implications. This approach enables clients to understand the full ramifications of what they are saying and generally results in a greater awareness of what is involved. Use of interpreting requires the HRD practitioner to draw a conclusion about the client's perception of a situation or event and is subject to error; that is, the interpretation could be incorrect. As a technique, interpreting provides a basis for publicly testing any assumptions made during a conversation. Thus it allows the client the opportunity to acknowledge the correctness of the HRD practitioner's interpretation as well as to verify his or her own point of view. Such common forms of statement as "What I hear you saying, . . ." and "Based upon what you have said, . . ." can be used by HRD practitioners to introduce their interpretations.

Paraphrasing. Using this technique, an HRD practitioner attempts to restate, in his or her own words, the client's basic message. The primary purpose of paraphrasing is to test the HRD practitioners's understanding of what has been said. Another purpose is to communicate to the client that the practitioner is trying to understand the client's basic message and, if the paraphrasing is successful, that the practitioner has been following what the client said. An example of paraphrasing would be: "You seem to be saying that his overbearing personality makes it difficult to accomplish the project."

Questioning. Questioning is a common and often overused communication technique. HRD practitioners should use questions only to obtain specifically needed information, or to direct the conversation with clients into more constructive and informative channels. Basically, there are two types of questions that are useful in selling: open- and closed-ended. Such questions may be directed at specific clients or at an entire group. While questions are often overused, they remain powerful tools with which to facilitate group discussion, guide the flow and direction of conversation, and help HRD practitioners obtain specific information very quickly.

Open-ended questions generally require more than a few words to answer and allow the client to expand the conversation in several different directions. They also help clients to widen their perceptual field and prepare them to consider divergent points of view. In short, open-ended questions may open the doors to developing a positive relationship and good rapport. An example might be for a HRD practitioner to ask a client, "Could you tell me how you feel about the quality of our training programs?" Several different approaches could be taken by clients in answering this type of question. While the practitioner is looking for a specific response, an open-ended question is less threatening to the client and allows that person to convey his or her point of view.

Closed-ended questions, in contrast, are ones that can be answered in relatively few words and have specific responses. They are important for gathering essential information, that is, for obtaining data needed as elements of the discussion between clients and HRD practitioners. This type of question also minimizes personal interaction. An example of a closed-ended question might be, "How long have you been in your current position?" This type of question is not concerned with the effectiveness of the response or the feelings of the client but rather with gathering needed information.

Silence. Although a somewhat difficult technique to master, the use of silence enables a client to think through what has transpired and provide additional information or explanations if appropriate or needed. It is important to remember that even experienced HRD practitioners are initially uncomfortable with silence as a technique. With practice, however, it becomes apparent that intentional silence provides clients with additional time to think about what they are going to say and allows them to explore their feelings more deeply. In addition, it may provide the less articulate clients with a feeling of worth. At the same time, silence can be overdone; more than a minute of silence, for example, will cause discomfort both to the client and to the HRD practitioner. Therefore, HRD practitioners will want to avoid extensive periods of silence because they may be misinterpreted and perceived as unresponsiveness. Silence is most useful when used in combination with other techniques such as encouraging and active listening.

Summarizing. HRD practitioners use this technique to convey to clients the essence of what has been said throughout the exchange. They may ask clients to agree or disagree with a summary in order to make certain that both sides were understood. An example of a summarizing statement would be, "Let me take a moment to summarize our conversation. . . ." Summarizing differs from paraphrasing in that it is used as the discussion with clients is drawing to an end. A summarizing technique deals with several thoughts and concepts. It also helps HRD practitioners determine the most appropriate steps to follow for each client. Alternatively, consultants may wish the clients to summarize the discussion. Again, this is a check for accuracy and understanding.

Reflecting. This technique consists of the HRD practitioner's bringing to the surface and verbalizing the emotional and/or substantive content of the client's words. Its purpose is to reveal that the HRD practitioner understands correctly what the client is feeling, thinking, or experiencing. It may actually verbalize the core of the client's attitude(s) that he or she has trouble putting into words.

Reflecting places the responsibility for feelings about and reactions to training with the person who has them. With it, the HRD practitioner can guide the conversation and bring out into the open feelings and hidden agendas. This is important because deeply hidden feelings can affect virtually every thought or behavior of a client. Such feelings often hinder the exchange process between clients and HRD practitioners, and so need to be brought to the surface in order to be dealt with effectively. This will help develop an open and honest exchange between clients and HRD practitioners. An example of a summarizing statement would be, "So you're looking for a training program that helps you develop interpersonal skills to help improve your effectiveness as a supervisor?"

Tentative Analysis. This is a "hunch" type of interpretation that does without definite cause-and-effect relationships. It is usually narrow in scope. A tentative analysis is usually stated in the form of a question because of its tentative nature. As such, it is a form of short summarization. It stops short of being comprehensive because it generally deals with one thought or concept instead of several. Its chief advantage is the way it communicates that an HRD practitioner is attempting to test publicly his or her understanding of client messages. By doing this one step at a time, the practitioner is demonstrating patience with and respect for the client's viewpoint. An example of tentative analysis would be, "I have a feeling you're not very satisfied with the quality of the sales training program."

These ten techniques will enable HRD practitioners to develop a comfortable working relationship with clients, one conducive to sharing ideas and feelings. Such a relationship is essential to the development of rapport with clients.

Phase 2: Discovering Performance Problems and Developmental Needs

Once a positive rapport with clients has been developed, HRD practitioners must turn their attention to discovering client performance problems and developmental needs. Having done so, they must help their clients estimate the seriousness of the performance problems and developmental needs facing them. Finally, they must determine if the client is willing to do something to correct these areas of deficiency.

The process of uncovering performance problems and developmental needs requires the use of each of the techniques previously discussed. The most useful ones are questioning (open and closed), reflecting, clarifying, active listening, encouraging, silence, and summarizing. All are directly linked to the communication process discussed in the opening section of Chapter Eight.

In order to discover the seriousness of a performance problem and/or developmental need we particularly recommend the use of four different types of questions. They are known as situation, problem, implication, and benefit questions (Rackham, 1988). Each will be addressed in detail.

Situation Questions. In Chapter Three, we identified a performance problem and/or developmental need as the difference between a client's current and desired states. Situation questions are designed to discover the current state of a client. They could be about the client's position or reporting relationship, the current performance level of the client's department or division, the number of people reporting to the client, the types of training programs the client or the client's people have participated in during the past two years, or, finally, the client's attitude toward HRD and its programs and services.

Situation questions establish a baseline for HRD practitioners. They let you know what the client is thinking and experiencing. They are also very safe and nonthreatening, easy to answer, and able to provide a platform for discussion. All this is very important during the early stages of a relationship, when rapport is fragile. Moving too quickly can jeopardize the new relationship.

Problem Questions. These are designed to discover the client's desired state. They can be direct or indirect. You can ask clients what performance problem they would like to have solved or which developmental needs they would like to have satisfied. If they will respond to such direct inquiries, by all means use them. But they can be very threatening, and so damage the relationship. Therefore, indirect inquiries are most recommended. You may want to ask clients what difficulties they are experiencing or what they are dissatisfied with. Such questions can be directed at their own or their employees' performance problems and developmental needs. Either way, this approach allows clients to indirectly describe their desired state.

Implication Questions. Neither situation nor problem questions provide HRD clients with an understanding of how serious their performance problems or developmental needs are. Implication questions are designed to help clients understand the seriousness and urgency by exploring the possible consequences. HRD practitioners take a performance problem or developmental need that the client perceives to be small and build it into a problem or need large enough to justify action.

They do this by posing a series of questions that identify the consequences of the problem. For example, the problem might be that a retail salesperson in the electronics department of a large department store is experiencing a 15 percent higher return rate of merchandise sold than the average for the department. Ask yourself what related difficulties this problem might lead to and write them down. These difficulties are the problem's implications. Five possible implication questions might provide insight into the seriousness of the problem, as well as help determine whether the problem is related to performance and/or skill deficiency or whether it is chiefly operational:

1. Are customers dissatisfied with the department service?
2. Is the salesperson qualifying customers to determine the type of merchandise that they want or need?
3. Is the salesperson using high-pressure closing techniques that result in sales but ultimately increase the number of returns?
4. Is the salesperson making claims about the merchandise that are not true?
5. Does the quality of the merchandise meet clients' expectations?

These questions will help the client understand that a 15 percent higher-than-average return rate can be a serious problem, one that results in future sales losses and a negative store image. The first four questions can be addressed through training interventions. The last, however, raises an operational issue that training cannot solve. Using implication questions will provide the client with a better understanding of the causes of performance problems and their consequences.

Benefit Questions. Once clients have learned the causes of performance problems and/or needs, HRD practitioners must determine if clients are willing to do something to correct them. In other words, they must ask questions that establish the value or usefulness of a solution. Questions of this type are referred to as benefit questions (Rackham, 1988). For instance, they might ask

- Is it important to you to solve this problem or meet this need?
- Why would you find this solution so helpful?
- Is there any other way this could help you?

The psychology of benefit questions is that they focus on the solution rather than the problem (Rackham, 1988). As a result, a positive problem-solving atmosphere is created. They also have the advantage of motivating the client to describe the benefits of a solution. Let us return to our previous example. The following are benefit questions that correspond to implication questions 1 to 5, previously mentioned.

1. Would you be interested in improving customer satisfaction?
2. How would training help salespeople improve their qualification techniques?
3. What benefits do you see in providing salespeople with training on closing techniques that are not considered high-pressure.
4. Would improved product knowledge help salespeople provide more accurate information about your merchandise? Why would that be helpful?

As you can see, all these questions have obvious answers—answers that each of us can provide. But the power of benefit questions is that it is the client who is providing the "reasons" for more and better training programs and HRD services. HRD practitioners must resist the temptation to provide the answers to clients. If they do resist it, clients will be much more supportive of training programs and HRD services that they themselves have identified as being critical.

We believe that the discovering phase is one of the important parts of the selling process. It is during this phase that clients share their needs and problems with HRD practitioners. This information allows the practitioners to communicate the advantages, benefits, and values of their training programs and services. In other words, the discovery phase provides an opportunity to communicate the value of HRD to the client. This is the beginning of the presentation process with the client.

The selling process as it has been described so far is outlined in Figure 9.2.

Phase 3: Presenting Solutions to Clients

Several years ago, Larry Wilson (former CEO of Wilson Learning Corporation and presently CEO of Pecos River Learning Center) revealed that the transition between the discovery phase and the presentation phase was one of the most difficult during the selling process. He believed that if you could make a simple statement communicating that your solution was based upon your client's needs, then the client would be willing to consider the solution seriously. He encouraged the use of the following phrase: "Based upon what you have told me, I would like to make the following recommendation." This simple sentence captures the meaning of the discovery phase and quickly moves you into the presentation phase.

During this phase of the selling process, HRD practitioners present solutions to clients. The phase consists of two parts: the *presentation* and *managing objections.*

How should HRD practitioners present solutions to clients?

The presentation should be based on the needs, interests, and expectations of the clients. The primary purpose of a presentation is to secure participation in HRD training programs or the use of HRD services. The solution(s) should be identified and presented in such a manner that the advantages, benefits, and values of the training programs and services can be understood by clients. This will demonstrate how the results desired by clients can be achieved. Let us look at each of these three components more closely.

Advantages. For each training program and service in the HRD program, you should identify the advantages and communicate them to clients when appropriate. For example, we have provided

Figure 9.2. The Process of SPIN Selling.

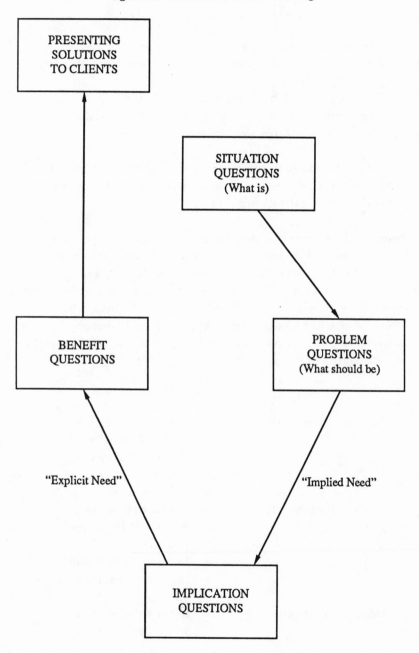

five advantages of a time management training program that could be so communicated. They are:

1. The program will help you prioritize your work.
2. The program will help you develop a systematic approach to planning projects.
3. The program will help you delegate effectively.
4. The program will improve your time allocation skills.
5. The program will help you manage interruption.

Clients who have identified time management as a cause of performance deficiencies would be interested in a training program that could produce these outcomes.

Benefits. Clients are also interested in knowing how a specific training program or HRD service will improve their performance or help satisfy their developmental needs. Therefore, it is not enough to identify the advantages of training programs and services. You must tell clients what the results will be. In other words, what is the benefit of new knowledge, added skills, or improved attitudes? Let us return to our previous example to illustrate the benefits of the time management program.

Advantage	*Benefit*
1. Prioritize your work	• Improved efficiency • Reduced overtime • Better utilization of resources • Reduced stress
2. Systematic approach to project planning	• Improved timeliness • Better coordination of activities • Improved profitability • Improved workload allocation
3. Delegate effectively	• Improved workload allocation

		• Improved efficiency
		• Helps develop human resources
		• More time to accomplish higher-priority tasks
4.	Time allocation skills	• Better time estimates
		• Better organization
		• Improved efficiency
		• Improved management of complex projects
5.	Manage interruption	• More personal time
		• Reduced stress
		• Improved quality time on priority tasks
		• Reduced resentment at heavy work load

Again, identification of benefits tells the client what improvement to expect as a result of participating in training programs or using HRD services. It is common to identify several benefits for each advantage listed.

Values. Finally, HRD practitioners must communicate the values of their training programs and services. Values should be expressed in terms of organizational improvements such as improved profitability, efficiency, productivity, and performance. By communicating the values of training programs and HRD services, HRD practitioners are communicating to clients why HRD is a vital part of the organization. Therefore, training programs and HRD services must be designed and developed in order to provide the values communicated.

HRD practitioners cannot communicate these values unless there is evidence to support their claims. In order to produce this evidence, practitioners must begin to conduct evaluations that will produce the cost-benefit data needed. This will require both impact and behavior evaluations. According to Brinkerhoff (1987), the cycle of performance improvement measurement begins with the design and implementation of correct evaluation strategies. Therefore, value communications begin with appropriate evaluation strategies too.

HRD practitioners must be careful not to overemphasize the values of training programs and HRD services. It would be better for them to communicate values that they can support than to establish expectations that cannot be met.

How should HRD practitioners manage clients' objections?

Each of the recommendations presented must include the advantages, benefits, and values that clients will receive. This will reduce the number of objections. However, objections will be voiced. When they are, HRD practitioners should not become defensive. Objections are simply questions that clients have about the training programs and HRD services. Above all, HRD practitioners should not argue with clients when they raise objections. Nor should they attack the client when overcoming an objection. At the same time, practitioners must not allow clients to answer their own objections because they may not answer them correctly. We have identified a four-step process for managing objections, as follows:

1. Acknowledge the objection.
2. Clarify the objection.
3. Problem-solve with the client.
4. Confirm the answer and get agreement that the objection was eliminated.

We call this the ACPC process from the initial letter of each step. Let us now look at it in more detail (Figure 9.3).

Acknowledging the Objection. This step consists of two activities: listening and sharing. Let us examine each of these separately.

Listening carefully to what a client is saying is the first step in managing objections. Usually, but not always, the client's words are an accurate reflection of what he or she is thinking. Most objections or negative statements are a way of verbalizing excess tension or fear. The very process of converting tension into words

Figure 9.3. The ACPC Model for Managing Objections.

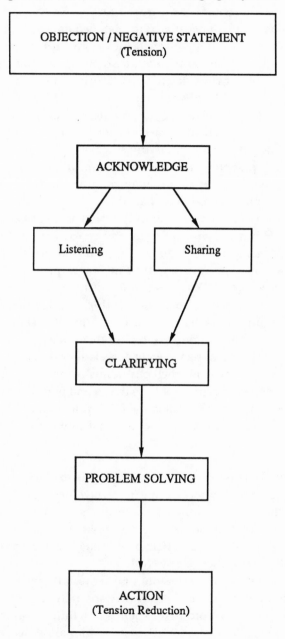

serves to reduce the tension, even if the words themselves do not actually reveal its nature or the reason for it.

An objection or negative statement deflates itself through the process of tension being converted into words, if they are allowed to flow uninterrupted. So the first, best, and easiest way to deflate an objection or negative statement is to listen to it, without interruption but with real and sincere interest.

What happens when HRD practitioners do not listen? Too often, they take the client's objections or negative statements as a personal attack. Instead of analyzing and diagnosing what the client is saying, the practitioners allow the statement to produce tension. However, they can learn to manage this tension successfully through the mutual process of sharing.

Sharing is a form of support. Tension as well as misery loves company. Human relations is our ability to share feelings with someone. Thus when HRD practitioners use words like "I understand how you feel," or "I guess I'm not surprised to find you feeling that way," or "You seem to feel strongly about that," they are reflecting and sharing someone's feelings. Real human relations is not a technique or skill, but a caring attitude. HRD practitioners help clients reduce tension by showing them that they understand how they feel, and that they are not surprised or upset.

When clients sense the consultants' confidence, it bolsters theirs. So to repeat and reemphasize the second part of the first step, our advice is to show clients that the HRD practitioners understand how they feel, and do or say nothing that might tend to increase their tension or fear.

Clarifying the Objection. The second step is to clarify the clients' thinking so that they are willing to receive new and logical evidence. If there is one thing known to human nature, it is that no one likes to look bad. So, when a client has raised an objection or made a negative statement, HRD practitioners have to make it easy for that client to withdraw gracefully.

Clients have to have reasons that are socially and emotionally acceptable to explain their behavior, especially changes in their behavior. There is a word that explains this thinking process; it is "rationalize." The dictionary defines "rationalize" as to ascribe one's acts, opinions, or decisions to causes that seem reasonable and valid, but are actually unrelated to the true cause of behavior. Strong emotional wants and desires do in fact influence most clients' decisions. But we know most clients do not like to admit this to themselves, much less to HRD practitioners.

Few HRD clients, then, are ready and willing to reveal the true motives behind their behavior, even when they understand what these are. They learn to cover them up with plausible reasons, explanations, and justifications, all designed to "prove" that they acted only after a well-thought-out and logical decision. This need to appear as a "rational creature" psychologically is a reflection of needs. People must be satisfied in their own minds that behavior is appropriate and justified. Often, they have to satisfy the thinking of others in order to win approval and forestall criticism. They need all the help they can get from consultants to do this successfully.

The challenge of answering objections or negative statements, then, is learning how to make an objection lose force without making a client lose face. That is why HRD practitioners have to help clients find reasons that are satisfactory to them.

When HRD practitioners have learned how to listen, share, and clarify, they will also have learned to remove the immature objection that is only a defense mechanism. They will have helped clients to again become open-minded and willing to listen. They will have recreated a positive climate and cleared the way to helping clients fulfill their needs.

Problem Solving with Clients. Once HRD practitioners have clarified an objection or negative statement, they are ready for the third step: actually answering the objection with key evidence. They will find problem solving easy if they train themselves to think, the client is asking me a question. What is it?

Keep in mind that the objection or negative statement clients give you is very often the one that they suspect someone else might be about to confront them with. Clients want to listen to how you would answer the objection. They want to determine if they can give the same answer to someone else. If clients can see themselves giving your answer, it is usually enough to satisfy others. Therefore,

everything HRD practitioners do or say must be based on empathy—on trying to imagine how the client feels.

Most objections and negative statements are centered around
three areas of concern:

- Will it work?
- Is it the best available?
- Will it be the best in the future?

If HRD practitioners provide answers that address these three areas
of concern, problem solving is about three-quarters accomplished.
The remaining part of problem solving is mutually working out
solutions to the clients' concerns.

Confirming the Answer. When a resolution is reached, HRD practitioners must make certain that the client is committed to taking
action to remedy the dispute. This is best accomplished by asking
for some kind of action. This is our fourth step in managing objections. It is no more difficult than that.

Phase 4: Supporting Clients' Decisions and Conclusions

This phase is often referred to as the *close*. A close is any actions that
imply or invite a commitment. In other words, it is anything that puts
the client in a position that involves making a decision. If HRD
practitioners have done an effective job of discovering performance
problems and developmental needs, have presented solutions that are
based on the client's problems and needs, and have managed objections effectively by using the ACPC approach, the most common
outcome is for clients to take action. So ask them to do so.

After clients have chosen to participate in a training program
or use an HRD service, HRD practitioners must perform three simple tasks:

1. *Support the client's decision.* This is because clients may
experience postdecision dissonance or dissatisfaction with their selection (see Chapter Three). Either of these conditions can result in
negative perceptions of HRD. During this phase, HRD practitioners' primary task is to obtain feedback from clients regarding their
feelings. If negative feedback is received, practitioners should apply
the ACPC model to reduce tension and provide answers. They

should use the feedback to adjust training programs and services. Practitioners should then report the changes to the client. This will help enhance the relationship.

2. *Manage the implementation of the selection.* This includes communicating with the client regarding the time and location of the training program, providing materials before the training program begins, delivering services in a timely fashion, reporting results quickly, and conducting posttraining discussions to determine if the training program helped improve performance or satisfied the developmental need. Another important consideration is to make certain that the new knowledge, skills, and/or behaviors have not been extinguished shortly after training. The risk of this can be reduced by scheduling follow-up activities and exercises that utilize the knowledge or skills or demonstrate the behaviors, or by scheduling meetings with the client for that purpose.

3. *Enhance the relationship with clients.* One way is for the HRD practitioner to establish a review committee consisting of executives, managers, supervisors, and employees. Such a committee would serve as subject matter experts and provide advice to the HRD program for a period of one or two years. It is possible that the training programs and services could be reviewed and recommendations made in order to improve their value to the organization. The committee could be viewed as an internal organization and known as the Friends of HRD. Committee members and HRD practitioners could meet regularly at breakfast or lunch and discuss the organization's performance problems and common developmental needs among employees. HRD practitioners might also try asking satisfied clients for names of other potential clients. This is known as the *referral method.* Besides its obvious usefulness to the HRD department, it also makes the clients who will provide the names into partners with the HRD program—a condition that reflects a very positive image of HRD and its practitioners.

Conclusion

This chapter has focused on the most effective promotional activity that HRD practitioners can utilize. While promotion is only one part of the marketing mix, it alone directly influences the decision making of HRD clients, and must be applied if marketing is to become an effective tool used for enhancing the image of HRD.

The most effective type of promotion is direct, face-to-face communications. We refer to this as personal selling, a process that consists of four critical steps designed to overcome clients' attitudes of no trust, no need, no help, and no support.

The selling process begins with establishing a rapport with clients. HRD practitioners must communicate their commitment and competence in order to reduce clients' resistance to HRD. In addition, practitioners should convey their goals for the call, establish an agenda, and set a time limit for the meeting.

During the second phase of the selling process HRD practitioners must uncover the needs of their clients. This can be accomplished through the use of four types of questions—situation questions, problem questions, implication questions, and benefit questions—designed to help HRD practitioners gauge the seriousness of their clients' problems and/or needs.

Once needs and/or problems have been uncovered, practitioners can present a solution. This phase of the selling process should be very straightforward and focused on solutions that help clients.

Finally, HRD practitioners must support the conclusions and actions of their clients. Obtaining feedback from them after a solution has been implemented will help determine if the client is satisfied. Another way to assure satisfaction is to make certain that the solution is correctly implemented and managed. The practitioner's accessibility to clients will help foster such an outcome.

Often clients will object to the solutions presented by HRD practitioners. If this occurs, practitioners should listen carefully and clarify what the objections are, then actively problem-solve with clients and determine if the answer presented reduces the clients' concerns. If an objection is handled correctly, acceptance of a solution is greatly enhanced.

Chapter Ten

Putting Plans into Action: Sixteen Steps for Marketing HRD Successfully

As you complete your study in marketing as it applies to HRD settings, it is appropriate to review the concepts we have developed in the first nine chapters. The first portion of this review will include a list of things to remember as you put your marketing knowledge to work. These will include a collection of suggestions gleaned from Chapters Two and Three that will help you integrate marketing principles into your work setting. This list will be followed by a review of the strategic marketing plan to remind you of the various principles of marketing. The review will also contain an adaptive discussion of the four major components of the marketing mix. Finally, you will be presented with a set of action steps. They will give you an idea of what you can do immediately to implement a structured marketing plan for your human resource development program.

Things to Remember

A marketing attitude is not an easy acquisition. It requires reorientation or a paradigm shift for most people, who are accustomed to giving customers what the marketers or sellers want to give them rather than what customers want. Adopting the attitude that the customer (client) is always right (even when wrong) is not an easy task. In many business roles, people are inclined to assume an adversarial relationship with clients or customers. Adoption of the

marketing concept requires that one's attitude shift to a client service mode. When adopting a marketing attitude one must *always*
remember that the human resource development enterprise is in
business only to serve clients, however defined. This decision is as
much attitudinal as it is cognitive. It is easy to memorize the elements of marketing but sometimes it is difficult to live them.

No More Body Count

The first of the things to remember when embarking on a marketing strategy is that the times of measuring the success of your HRD
effort by the numbers of people completing its programs have def-
initely passed. From now on, the measure of success of any such
program will be whether or not it satisfied the needs of its clients.
It is a change that involves a very different orientation for many
HRD professionals, who for years have been inclined to do their
reporting and measure their accountability by the numbers of their
customers or the hours spent in their classes and programs. They
have had a difficult time with measures of success based on outcomes, and so have, instead, spent their energies adding up the
numbers associated with their offerings. For a human resource development professional, this will not do. You must determine what
your customers want, get it in writing, and go about satisfying that
need. Your accountability measures must be developed in terms of
measuring that satisfaction, usually in the form of behavior change.

Talk Their Language

Many HRD professionals have been acculturated in the vernacular
of education. They can talk about cognitive development, Piagetian
theory, or reinforcement principles, and cite and use a hundred
educational acronyms. This is not appropriate. Learners in a business setting are accustomed to a business vocabulary and should not
be subjected to the multiplicity of academic vocabulary. That is not
to say that appropriate educational terms should not be used occasionally. But to flood clients with words that are alien to their day-
to-day existence will not add to an HRD professional's prestige.

Be Service Oriented

As we alluded to earlier, the marketing concept suggests that the whole human resource development enterprise is in business to satisfy clients' needs. This should be what drives the organization; this service-oriented attitude should pervade the HRD group from top to bottom and side to side. It should be evident to anybody observing the actions and agenda of the HRD program that it is in business to satisfy clients by changing behavior. This is how its practitioners will be judged and this is how they will be successful.

Don't Forget the Exchange of Value

One of the most important principles in the realm of marketing is known as the exchange process. Some believe that it is as important as the marketing concept. The exchange process is the offering of value to another party in return for something of value. Simply put, you must deliver value, as seen by clients, that is equal to the time and energy that they commit to your activity. If they do not receive or perceive that they receive benefits that equal their commitment, they will believe that an equal exchange has not occurred and will not be satisfied clients. Your goal is to not just develop exchanges that are equal, but to develop exchanges in which clients believe that they received more than they gave in the form of commitment. In order for this to happen, you must constantly remember the exchange concept and become skilled at understanding, planning, and managing exchange.

The Adoption Process Is Alive and Well

Your human resource development clients will go through a predictable series of stages, steps, or events as they consider adopting or participating in a training program or other HRD service. Either they or their supervisor will become aware of a performance problem or a need. This stage will be followed by an interest in looking at alternatives to satisfy that need. Your clients will then evaluate the alternatives available to them and select one. Several approaches may be available through your programs. Finally, they will formally adopt an alternative and decide to participate in the training program or service. You must understand this process and be attentive to it at all times. You should always know where you and your clients are in the adoption process. By knowing, you can facilitate the movement of clients through the adoption process and you will experience attendant success in your HRD program.

The You of You

It is no accident that marketers use well-known and/or respected people to provide testimonials for their products. They are frequently selling the personality of the testifier in addition to (or in some cases in place of) the product or service they have to provide. We are not suggesting that HRD professionals should use well-known people to tout their services. You should understand, however, that clients frequently buy confidence in addition to products or services. The level of confidence that you exude in your HRD program will be directly reflected in the level of acceptance of that program by your clientele. Don't ignore the fact that your programs are being judged, in part, by how you present them.

Reviewing the Strategic Marketing Plan

As you learned in Chapter Four, the strategic marketing plan is the centerpiece of the marketing activity for those who have adopted the marketing concept. This plan includes a predictable set of steps that must be followed. Its given features are that the marketing concept must be adopted and the exchange process must be understood. The plan embodies the theory and practice of marketing and is endorsed by academic as well as marketing wisdom. In order to put marketing skills into action, a specific plan must be followed.

It is well known that little will happen in any enterprise without a plan. Marketing is certainly no exception to this rule. The plan must begin with a statement of intentions or expectations and conclude with a description of actions that are in turn accountable to the important publics.

The marketing plan is always driven by a marketing mission statement, which would be the first activity associated with the plan. The next activity, called a situational analysis, begins to get at the real meat of the plan. The marketing planner in the realm of human resource development must look within and to the outside of the organization for input into the planning process, and that planning must take into account the situation surrounding the marketing function and be cognizant of the forces that affect it.

The next mainline activity in the marketing plan is the development of more specific marketing goals and objectives for the human resource development enterprise. These goals grow from the mission statement and are responsive to the environment described in the situational analysis. This activity is followed by market research on appropriate market segments. Finally, the elements of the marketing mix are developed to complete the marketing plan.

The Marketing Mission Statement

The marketing mission statement is frequently described in rather lofty and general terms. There is talk of the philosophical and ideological goals, objectives, and underpinnings embraced by the organization, while some general hint is given regarding expected outcomes. In such a statement, vagueness is to be tolerated. Organizations must have a general mission statement from which a marketing mission statement can be extrapolated.

The creation of a strategic marketing plan for human resource development begins with the formulation and statement of the organization's mission. A mission statement would typically answer questions such as, What is our purpose? Who are our clients? What do we have that is of value for clients? What will our purpose be in the future? It acts as a guide, helping to shape and form the activities of the organization's members. It may give some indication regarding who is to be served and satisfied, and in what ways. It needs to be responsive to clients and to the organization. The mission statement should make clear that the organization is embracing the marketing concept.

The Situational Analysis

As we have said earlier, almost nothing occurs in a vacuum. This is true of businesses and institutions that harbor an HRD organization. Marketing, by its very nature, is a function that occurs within a larger social environment. It must be clearly stated what that environment is and who it includes.

Normally we think in terms of external environments that include financial conditions, managerial attitudes, competitors, and images. These environments need to be analyzed and recognized. They might also include economic conditions, legal and political realities, state of technology, and availability of resources.

Environments internal to the organization must also be considered by the HRD manager who is developing a strategic marketing plan. The least extensive of these environments would be people engaged directly in human resource development within the organization. More broadly speaking, internal environments might include persons at work within the organization, financial conditions, managerial attitudes, and facilities available, as well as the organization's image. Each of these items plus several more, as delineated in Chapter Four, might be considered when creating the environmental analysis that will undergird the marketing plan.

Researching the Market

In order for an HRD group to adopt the marketing concept, its members must understand as much as possible about the market in question. In order to understand that market they must empirically study it. There are many ways to learn the needs of a clientele, and these ways are generally categorized under the heading of market research. No longer can organizations develop products and/or services and naively introduce them to a mass market. The only viable strategy for being responsive to a market is to engage in a careful process of market research. It involves the orderly acquisition and analysis of data that measure some component of the marketing system for the purpose of improving an organization's marketing decisions. It can involve experiments, surveys, focus groups, interviews, and a wide range of other strategies.

Market research is a systematic process that follows the five steps typically known as the scientific method. They include identifying and defining the problem, developing hypotheses, collecting data, interpreting the findings, and developing the research report.

Following these steps will ensure a legitimate attempt to assess the wants and needs of the clients.

Segmenting the Market

Market segmentation is based on the fact that client and or customer preferences are often clustered in groups or segments. These are sometimes called niches. It is prudent for the marketing professional to identify these segments and work to satisfy their individual and unique needs.

Markets can be segmented in an assortment of ways including geographical, demographic, psychographic, and behavioral. Once these segments are identified, the efforts to market in them are called target marketing. Human resource development marketers who carefully delineate and examine their markets are bound to experience a greater degree of success in terms of acceptance of their programs and movement toward the achievement of the organizational mission.

Cost-Benefit Strategy for the HRD Program

Pricing in human resource development takes on a broader definition than the narrowly economic one. Many HRD practitioners make the mistake of discounting the importance of price when developing and planning courses and activities. Certainly, in order to meet clients' needs, price must be a consideration.

Price, in this context, is the value placed on what is exchanged. Something of value—usually purchasing power—is exchanged for satisfaction or utility. Price is probably the most flexible of the variables in the marketing mix, that is, marketers can usually adjust their prices more easily and quickly than they can change the other variables. It may not, however, be appropriate to change the price if the indicators from market research do not suggest that change.

As was suggested earlier, marketers are accustomed to thinking of price in terms of monetary measures. But prices in the realm of human resource development can take on characteristics in addition to monetary ones; for instance, they may include a collection of what are known as perceived costs. These may be such costs as time spent, risk taken, social capital used, energy expended, resources used, or other costs that may amount to negative outcomes or depletion of resources possessed by the client.

After the marketing objectives have been stated, the HRD organization can begin to consider an appropriate price. The available pricing strategies may tend to fall into three or four categories, including cost oriented, demand oriented, or competition oriented, or some combination of these. There are several steps associated with setting prices for an HRD program. They include developing pricing objectives, determining the market's amenability to price, determining demand, comparing demand, cost, and profit, examining competitors' prices, selecting a pricing policy, selecting a pricing method, and selecting the price.

Finally, after selecting a pricing policy, the HRD marketer should choose a pricing method, which is a mechanical strategy for setting prices on a regular basis. The nature of the program, together with the volume and number of programs delivered by the organization, will help to determine how these prices are calculated. Marketers must consider pricing approaches as well as knowledge about clients, demand, costs, and competition.

Time/Location Strategy for Human Resource Development

A time/location strategy involves getting the right programs to the target market at the right time. A program will not be useful to a client if it is not available when and where it is wanted and needed. The variables associated with this strategy include location of training—whether or not it is on the job, in a formal classroom setting, off the job, and/or independent or self-directed study—as well as facilities in which training takes place. A comfortable and supportive environment should be considered when training programs are designed and developed, as well as when they are delivered. Other location strategies include time of day, method of instruction, and physical environment of the courses to be offered.

The basic distribution question for an HRD organization is, How can programs be made available and accessible to clients? Particular attention should be paid to this notion of availability in order to make certain that courses are accessible to the people who want to take them. In terms of distribution objectives, the most basic question to answer is, What level of convenience should be offered to the enrollees? Obviously cost will be an issue, but the HRD department might try to describe the maximum level of service it could offer. No matter what kind of facility is chosen, the most important element is the extent to which the facility will add to or detract from consumer satisfaction.

Promotional Strategy for Human Resource Development

Promotion is among the most popular, well-known, and well-developed of the elements of the marketing mix. Everyone thinks he or she knows about promotion; almost no one does. For the purposes of this discussion, promotion can be divided into two categories: sales promotion, and personal selling. Basically, promotion is a communication process. Communication is made up of six elements, namely, the source of communication, a message, a medium of communication, a receiver of the message, a return of the message (feedback), and barriers to communication. When promotional strategies are used, they will include some reference to these elements.

Promotional strategies can be widely varied. Many HRD professionals are afflicted with what we have termed "brochure lust": they believe that promotion begins and ends with the development of a brochure to describe a program. Nothing could be further from the truth. Promotion should begin with determining the objective associated with promoting a given program, and be followed eventually with a decision regarding what medium should be employed to spread the promotional message. That might include personal selling, information in a company house organ, a television program, or even the development and dissemination of a brochure.

The purposes of promotion are to inform, persuade, or remind clients of the advantages, benefits, and values of training programs and services. This is what should be foremost in the minds of HRD professionals as they develop promotional strategies for their programs. The factors affecting the selection of promotional activities include the nature of training programs and services, the marketing objectives of the HRD program, the program strategy, and the HRD budget. Promotion can be used to improve the credibility of the human resource development function. It may also help to encourage greater participation in training programs, to educate clients regarding improvements in training programs and services, and to stabilize a fluctuating demand for programs.

There are barriers to success in the overall promotion of HRD. They include a lack of trust, a feeling that training is not needed, a feeling that training will not and has not helped, and a feeling that there is no support for a person to engage in training activity.

A great deal of the promotional energy associated with an HRD marketing strategy will be in the form of personal selling, that is, personally convincing members of the client group that the HRD program is appropriate to the needs of the client group. The wise HRD professional will find a current book on modern selling, read the book, and apply the principles to his or her HRD enterprise.

Action Steps for Marketing HRD Programs

The implementation of a strategic marketing plan begins with the identification of critical action steps. We have identified sixteen action steps as appropriate for HRD practitioners in the design, development, and implementation of a strategic marketing plan. Each action step has been designed to help you develop one or more of the components of a strategic marketing plan. We will describe each of the action steps and provide a brief explanation of the procedures in which you can engage to accomplish it.

Step 1: Adopt a Service-Oriented Attitude

The first action step that HRD practitioners must take is the adoption of a service-oriented attitude. In Chapter One the importance of the marketing concept to the creation of a successful strategic marketing plan was identified. The marketing concept demonstrates that HRD practitioners must develop a service-oriented approach to meeting the needs of their clients. The first step in the creation of a service-oriented approach is the development of a service-oriented attitude. In other words, HRD practitioners must place the needs and wants of their clients above their own needs and wants. In addition, the step requires HRD practitioners to focus on serving the needs of their client base. An attitude that is service-oriented simply implies that HRD practitioners provide training programs and services that help improve the performance as well as satisfy the developmental needs of their clients. It implies listening to clients and their demands. It implies working with clients in the identification of a collaborative HRD program.

Accomplishing this step requires the HRD practitioner to do an internal audit, that is, to complete some reflective activities that allow one to be honest regarding one's general attitude toward clients. A helpful activity here is to write down why you are currently involved in the HRD field within your organization. Once you have completed a comprehensive list, try to isolate a central theme. Once it has been identified, the following criteria can be used to determine whether there is a positive, service-oriented attitude toward clients in your department:

- Are *you* interested in improving and enhancing the personal or professional development of others?
- Are *you* interested in improving the profitability and effectiveness of the organization?
- Are *you* interested in addressing issues, problems, and ideas in a collaborative manner?
- Are *you* generally interested in the enhancement of people and their skills, knowledge, or behavior?
- Are *you* interested in the development of programs and/or services that can be viewed by members of the organization as critical to the accomplishment of their goals and objectives?

It would be appropriate to examine the list to determine if at least two of these five criteria can be applied. If none apply, examine the attitude that exists toward clients and the organization.

An HRD practitioner who fails to take an interest in the enhancement of individuals, groups, and/or the organization will certainly not possess the type of attitude that is appropriate for enhancing the image of HRD. Furthermore, an HRD practitioner who does not score positively on a majority of these criteria will most likely have a tendency to be self-serving. This will not allow the HRD programs to become responsive to the needs of clients.

Step 2: Create an Exchange Process

The exchange process is the offering of value to another party in return for equal or greater value. This definition is critical to the enhancement and improvement of the image of HRD, whose practitioners must be able to articulate the value of each of their training programs and services and communicate it to prospective clients.

At this stage, you should identify

- The training programs and services that are offered clients
- The values that can be received as a result of participation in each
- How best to communicate these values to potential clients

This can be done by constructing a sentence or two that describes the values to be exchanged with a potential client for each of the training programs and services offered. As a result, the activities and elements of your training program, but more importantly the values that the client will receive from it, will be communicated.

Another pertinent activity would be to create a three-way exchange model similar to the one in Chapter Two, as follows:

1. Identify the names of your HRD program, your organization, and the clients that exchange with the program.
2. Identify the values exchanged with the clients as well as the values exchanged with the organization.
3. Identify the values that the clients and the organization will exchange as a result of participation in the training programs and/or services.
4. Identify what the client and the organization will exchange with each other.

At the completion of these four steps, a counterclockwise and a clockwise loop with the HRD department, the clients of HRD, and the organization will have been created. The final step in the three-way exchange process is to identify the outcomes of a successful exchange. This model should be used as a guide to help in communicating the importance and criticality of HRD or management as well as to individual HRD clients.

Step 3: Conduct an Audit of Your Training Programs and Services

An ideal way of determining whether the organization has created training programs and services that are needs based is to conduct an audit of existing training programs and services. Such an audit should reveal the nature of the training program, its purpose, its outcomes, and the potential organizational impact that could be realized as a result of it. A representative sample of HRD clients should then be assembled in small focus groups of no greater than eight and charged with the responsibility of determining if the training programs or services represented meet the needs of their constituencies. At the completion of the focus groups, HRD practitioners should compare their audit with the list identified by the focus group participants. This is done in order to determine if there is a positive correlation between the two. If there is, it could be concluded that the training programs and services developed by the HRD program are based upon the needs of the clients within the organization. If, however, there is a negative correlation, the HRD practitioners should examine their training programs and services to determine what can be done to make them more client focused.

Another positive outcome of this type of audit is that the individuals in the focus groups can serve as internal advocates for the HRD program. Such "ambassador relationships" are extremely difficult to cultivate, but once created are very valuable for improving the image of HRD.

Step 4: Identify the Demand State of Clients Within the Organization

In Chapter Two, we identified a number of demand states that may face HRD programs. Each state has unique characteristics and can affect the image of HRD in many ways. Therefore, HRD practitioners must be aware of the demand state that they are currently facing within the organization.

Step 4 is designed to help you identify that state. This can be accomplished by using other focus groups, or through questionnaires and/or interviews. Once an appropriate data collection strategy has been found, a list of questions to obtain information from the representative audience should be developed. Questions should be focused on the type of demand state that currently exists. A careful review of the demand states identified in Chapter Two would also be in order before this list of questions is completed.

The goal of this particular activity is to identify the needs of various constituent groups within the organization. It is important to remember that different groups within the organization may maintain entirely different demand states. Therefore, it is critical to use data collection methods that can be applied to all constituent groups but are still flexible enough and detailed enough to identify all possible characteristics of demand states within the organization.

Step 5: Adopt a Marketing Response Appropriate to the Demand State(s) Identified

Step 5 is designed to help identify the most appropriate marketing response to the demand states previously identified. First, you should review the marketing responses identified in Chapter Two for the demand states that you have been able to uncover within your organization. Once the possible marketing responses have been reviewed, it is important to begin to create a plan of action that will result in positive outcomes. The exact steps to follow in response to the demand state or states will be addressed during later action steps in this chapter.

Step 6: Review the Adoption Process and Innovativeness

In Chapter Three, the phases of the adoption process were identified. HRD clients face many decisions every day; some are simple and routine, requiring little effort, while others are difficult and complex, requiring much. Action step 6 begins with a review of the phases of the adoption process:

- Awareness of performance problems and developmental needs
- Developing interest
- Evaluating alternatives
- Selecting an alternative
- Adopting an alternative and evaluating the selection

Each of these steps examines and considers training programs and services. Simply stated, the adoption process is a five-phase approach to the selection and evaluation of training programs and services. It is critical to approach the introduction of new training programs as well as existing programs with each of these five phases clearly understood.

Another important concept introduced in Chapter Three was that people differ in their response to the training programs and services offered by HRD practitioners. Five different types of individuals who participate in training programs and services were identified: the innovator, the early adopter, the early majority, the late majority, and the laggards. Each of these types of individuals has unique characteristics and buying patterns associated with their adoption of training programs and services. The most important part of this action step is the review of the adoption process and of the innovativeness of clients within the organization. Once this has been conducted, an appropriate promotional strategy can be created as part of the strategic marketing planning process.

Step 7: Create a Marketing Mission Statement for Your HRD Program

A marketing mission statement can serve as a way of organizing HRD practitioners within the organization around a common outcome. It can also serve as a guide to help HRD practitioners in decision making. This can include both decisions on the types of activities that HRD practitioners engage in and decisions on the focus of the HRD program. In 1990, the American Society for Training and Development (ASTD) developed a book series called

Trainers Tool Kit. One of the first books to be published in it was titled "Mission Statements for HRD Programs." This book included sample mission statements from a multitude of different organizations and HRD journals. Here are some examples (Olivetti, 1990):

1. *AT&T corporate education:* The corporate education and training organization supports AT&T's need to improve learning opportunities for customers and employees by delivering a wide range of programs and courses worldwide through partnerships with all education and training groups in AT&T (p. 7).

2. *Metropolitan Transit Commission:* The training center exists to encourage learning at the Metropolitan training center. Our mission is based on the belief that continuing learning is critical to providing better service to the public and a positive work environment for employees (p. 81).

3. *Mayo Foundation:* To develop and maintain a management training and development program that will: support Mayo Foundation's goals and objectives; utilize the combined resources of the Foundation; provide management and development services designed to meet the identified and evolving needs of all Foundation entries and management staff. Recognize and support the management and development requirements unique to a single Foundation entry (p. 77).

4. *William M. Mercer, Incorporated:* The corporate professional development group provides internal consulting services to enhance performance for individuals and groups. We do this through the application of performance interventions which enhance employee satisfaction and growth, improve efficiency, competitiveness and profitability (p. 143).

The mission statements serve to focus the role that the HRD program has within each organization. In addition, they communicate the types of interventions and strategies to be used by an HRD program in order to improve the efficiency, profitability, and competitiveness of the organization. A mission statement, then, should serve as a guide to the development of goals and objectives for the HRD program.

We have already shown how important it is to create a marketing mission statement for the HRD program. A guide to creating one should include five things:

- The name of your group
- The role that HRD practitioners will serve in the organization (internal consultant, trainer, instructional designers and so on)
- The type of population served
- The types of interventions to be employed by the HRD program
- The types of outcomes desired as a result of the interventions

Each of these five should be included in the creation of the mission statement.

Step 8: Conduct a Situation Analysis of the Environment and Analyze the Organizational Culture

In Chapter Four, we stressed the importance of creating an internal and external environmental analysis within the organization. This analysis was designed to help uncover opportunities and constraints that currently exist within the organization and the strengths and weaknesses of the HRD program. There were a number of areas to be considered when conducting an external environmental analysis:

- Economic conditions of the organization
- Legal-political environment
- Sociocultural values of the organization
- Technological state of the organization
- Resources available to the organization
- Competitive structure of the organization

From this list one should identify the constraints and opportunities that face the HRD program. This will greatly help HRD practitioners allocate financial and human resources.

The areas that must be considered for an internal environmental analysis are

- Financial condition of the organization
- Managerial attitudes and abilities
- Condition of present facilities
- Personnel quality and quantity
- HRD's current competitive position
- HRD's organizational image
- Degree of centralized versus decentralized structure within the organization

Each of these seven should be used to identify the strengths and weaknesses of the HRD program.

The third phase of a situational analysis is to identify the various dimensions of the organizational culture. This is done by a narrative description of the cultural environment that exists within the organization and should include

- Hierarchical structure of the organization
- Managerial style present within the organization
- Degree of autonomy and freedom within the organization
- Accessibility to upper management
- Type of decision-making procedures and policies used within the organization
- Reward system currently in place
- Compensation program within the organization
- Organization's attitude toward human resources

These will help you construct a good overall picture. All current and future marketing activities must take into account the existing organizational culture.

Conducting internal and external environmental analyses as well as an organizational cultural analysis will result in the collection of a great deal of information about the organization that you represent. The constraints on the HRD program will become obvious; the program's strengths and weaknesses and a composite of the organizational culture will be clearly identified. These three will combine to provide information about the types of individuals within the organization and the type of organization you represent. They will help you create an appropriate set of strategies to affect both.

Step 9: Create Goals and Objectives for the HRD Program

The next step in the creation of a strategic marketing plan is to identify the HRD program's goals and objectives. This is a very simple and straightforward activity. Simply identify the goals to accomplish as a result of the program, then identify its objectives or outcomes. The latter should be broad in nature and in scope. They should encompass the holistic outcomes that must be accomplished within a specific time frame.

Once the goals have been identified, attention should be turned to the creation of specific objectives. Objectives are a microcosm of the goals. They should be written in measurable and specific terms and be realistic and obtainable. They should also be written for a short time frame such as six months or a year. They are small steps to the accomplishment of the HRD program's goals.

Step 10: Create a Market Research Program for HRD

As you review Chapter Five, it is important to realize that a market research program is simply a form of needs assessment within the organization. Market research is absolutely critical to the creation of an HRD program that will be responsive to the needs of clients. It is also important to understanding and affecting the exchange process within the organization. Therefore, market research is critical to adhering to the two fundamental laws of marketing.

Many HRD practitioners feel ill equipped to deal with market research as a activity within their HRD program. To overcome this apprehension, ASTD has produced two monographs that are helpful in the creation of a market research program: *How to Collect Data* (Gilley, 1990) and *Statistics for HRD Practitioners* (Martelli and Mathern, 1991). They outline the characteristics of an effective HRD research program and explain how to utilize statistics in evaluating the data collected.

Step 11: Identify a Target Market for
Training Programs and Services

The first purpose of this action step is for HRD practitioners to identify the most appropriate target markets for each of their training programs and services. The second purpose is to identify the most appropriate market segments for each of their training programs and services. These two purposes can be realized when HRD practitioners combine the training programs and services they offer with those of the various market segments that currently exist within their organization. This can be done by constructing a matrix that identifies all the HRD interventions (that is, all training programs and services) and all the marketing segments. It should be remembered that marketing segments can include roles within the organization, types of job classifications, titles, or any combination of these. List the HRD interventions on the left-hand side of a page and the marketing segments at the top. Once the matrix has been constructed, simply identify which marketing segment would be most appropriate for the corresponding intervention. Working through this matrix, an HRD practitioner can get a picture of how many different marketing segments are represented by each intervention. This will help construct training programs and services that are focused on either a single marketing segment or some combination of marketing segments.

Step 12: Conduct a Program/Service Audit as a Way
of Creating a Program/Service Strategy

One of the most critical action steps is the development of a program/service audit for the HRD program. First, identify all of the current HRD interventions that the program offers. This should include training programs, services, consulting activities, and seminars and conferences. Next, construct a concept life cycle similar to that in Figure 6.1. This diagram should help place the interventions in either the exposure, acceptance, maturity, or decline phase of the concept life cycle. After completing a concept life cycle for all of the interventions, it is important to construct a portfolio analysis for each. This should be similar to the one found in Figure

6.4. Each intervention should be identified as either a Super Star, a Wandering Star, a Constant Star, or a No Star. This exercise will require judgment as to the applicability as well as the importance of various HRD interventions.

Once a program life cycle and a portfolio analysis have been constructed, construct a model that is similar to Figure 6.5. The purpose of this model is to combine the concept life cycle and the portfolio analysis in such a way as to create a strategy for each of the HRD interventions identified. One of four strategies—build, hold, harvest, or divest—should be identified. As a way of review, consider the phase of the concept life cycle that an HRD intervention is currently in; then consider its portfolio position; and then move to the far right of Figure 6.5 to identify the appropriate strategy for each intervention. On your first draft, it is important to simply identify the strategies without a great deal of thought and consideration. During a second and third draft it will be important to seriously consider either the concept life cycle position or the portfolio position before identifying an exact strategy. Take into account the size of the organization, the marketing segmentation model created previously, and the amount of available resources identified during the environmental analysis. Based on that additional information, you will be able to find the exact appropriate strategy.

Once a strategy has been constructed for each of the HRD interventions, you can implement a program/service strategy for your HRD program, as follows:

1. Determine which programs and services are considered to be Super Stars, Wandering Stars, or Constant Stars appropriate for additional resources.
2. Identify the Wandering Stars and the Constant Stars to maintain a current level of resource allocation.
3. Identify the Constant Stars, Wandering Stars, and No Stars that would begin to reduce the human resource and financial allocations.
4. Identify the programs to discontinue.

You now have a program/service strategy that should serve as the foundation for the strategic marketing plan from this point forward.

Step 13: Develop a Cost-Benefit Strategy for the HRD Program

One of the most important parts of a strategic marketing planning process is the identification of a cost-benefit analysis strategy. Such a strategy demonstrates the relationship between the costs and the benefits of training programs and services—a relationship that can serve as the promotional message to be communicated to decision makers and upper management. A cost-benefit strategy begins with the identification of all potential costs incurred as a result of the design, development, and implementation of training programs and services. These include

- Employees' salaries
- Design costs
- Development costs
- Material costs
- Media costs
- Hotel and meeting rooms costs
- Travel costs
- Lost opportunity cost (loss of productivity by participating employees)
- Promotional material (advertising, program catalogs, and so forth)
- Travel and per diem expenses for participants and instructors

Each of these costs should be collected for every training program, service, and HRD intervention provided by the HRD program.

It is very difficult to operationalize the benefits received from training programs and services. Nevertheless, it is important that they should be identified. They include improved profitability, increase in revenue, increase in sales, reduction in personnel turnover, improvement in time savings, improvement in product quality, reduction in maintenance and operational costs, improvement in attitudes and behavior, and improvement in organizational morale.

Figures 10.1 and 10.2 represent a sample of a cost-benefit analysis conducted at William M. Mercer. Figure 10.1 outlines the possible costs incurred as a result of a time management course taught to 166 consultants in the second and third quarters of 1990. Figure 10.2 identifies the cost savings using two different methods. Panel A reflects the cost savings realized to the organization as calculated by an hourly rate method. Such a method accounts for the savings that can occur based upon the hourly salary rate of the participants. Panel B reflects the savings that can be realized when you use a billing rate calculation. This method is used in professional service firms to reflect the average billing rate per consultant per hour. Regardless of which method is used, the organization is shown to have realized a substantial savings as a result of this training program.

The results of the cost-benefit analysis should be communicated to upper management and/or decision makers within the organization to reflect the improved opportunity cost as a result of HRD. This type of analysis is an excellent way of enhancing and improving the credibility of HRD within the organization. If such cost-benefit analyses are conducted for all training programs and services, one can quickly realize that HRD is not a cost but in reality an investment that produces positive results. Such information can be used as a powerful message in promotional communications to organization decision makers.

Figure 10.1. Components of Cost/Benefit Analysis.

- Duration of course: 16 hours
- Number of employees who participated: 166
- Cost: $400 per participant
- Average annual compensation for 166 participants: approximately $75,000
- Average hourly compensation: approximately $40 (40 hours per week for 48 weeks)
- Average number of weeks worked per year: 48
- Average number of hours saved per week: 2.08

Figure 10.2. Cost/Benefit Analysis of Time-Management Course: Hourly Rate Method.

COSTS

Hours for course	×	Number of participants	×	Average hourly rate	=	Subtotal	+	(Course cost	×	Number of participants)	=	Total cost
16	×	166	×	$40	=	$106,240	+	(400	×	166)	=	$172,640

SAVINGS

Average hourly rate	×	Average hours saved per week	×	Number of weeks worked	×	Number of participants	=	Savings
$40	×	2	×	48	×	166	=	$637,440

COST/BENEFIT

	Savings	-	Total cost	=	Total savings
	$637,440	-	$172,640	=	$464,800

Using a billing rate method would increase the savings proportionately. Billing rates average approximately 2.5 times the hourly salary. This would increase savings to $1,162,000.

Step 14: Create a Time/Location Strategy

Creating a time/location strategy is a very simple, straightforward activity that should include identifying the time, place, and location of all training programs and services. One should also take into account the size of the organization, how it is structured, its geographic dispersion, the number of employees in given locations, the size of the HRD staff, and the financial resources available to the HRD program. These should help account for the type of time and location strategy developed.

Each training program and service should be carefully examined in relationship to the time and location strategy to see if it is congruent with the organization's demographic and geographic dispersion. In essence, a time/location strategy is a way of checking to see if indeed the HRD program and its practitioners are practicing the marketing concept. Some HRD programs offer training programs during times and in places that are convenient to the HRD staff and comfortable to its budget. Such an approach reflects neither a responsive HRD program nor the importance of meeting client needs and being focused on client satisfaction. While it is important to maintain an appropriate budget and be concerned with the needs of the HRD practitioners, it is more important to be focused on the concerns of the HRD clients. A time/location strategy should be written in such a way as to embrace client needs and demonstrate the characteristics of a responsive HRD program.

Step 15: Develop a Promotional Strategy
for the HRD Program

The development of a promotional strategy for an HRD program consists of six separate but interrelated activities. Each of these activities was thoroughly discussed in Chapters Eight and Nine.

1. Identify the Constraints. The process begins with the identification of the barriers to communication. This will enable an HRD practitioner to understand what kinds of constraints must be faced in implementing a promotional strategy.

2. Apply the AIDA Model. Next, HRD practitioners should utilize the AIDA model outlined in Chapter Eight. AIDA stands for awareness, interest, desire, and action. Awareness of training programs and services is the first step in the communication process. The message that is created by HRD practitioners regarding their training programs and services must include an outline of the training program, with the activities and outcomes that result from participation. But, most importantly, the values of each training program and service must also be communicated. If they are, HRD clients should want to participate in training programs or utilize services. Once HRD clients' interests have been aroused, the communication process should enhance their desire to take action; it might tell them, for example, how a training program can improve a performance problem or satisfy a developmental need of theirs. Finally, HRD clients should be motivated by the communication process to take some kind of action to meet that difficulty or need.

3. Create a Sales Promotion Program. Third, HRD practitioners should create a sales promotion program that reflects the image they desire. The program should include creation of appropriate HRD program catalogs, brochures, information pieces, and promotional memorabilia. It will also do well to include the logos and program colors as well as letterhead and stationery. The idea behind such a program is to arouse interest in as well as identification with the HRD program. A self-promotion program should also be focused on distributing a common message to a variety of marketing segments within the organization.

4. Recruit Internal Advocates. One of the best ways to improve and enhance the image of HRD within the organization is to identify and recruit internal advocates for the HRD program. This process consists of identifying centers of influence as well as opinion leaders who have the ability to communicate the values of HRD to others in the organization. The individuals who are identified and ultimately recruited as internal advocates should have appropriate positional power within the organization and/or an opportunity to influence key decision makers within the organization. They should also maintain high visibility as well as credibility within the organization, and be able to articulate the mission and purpose of HRD as well as its goals and objectives. In other words, internal advocates should serve as spokespersons for HRD in the organization. With that in mind, it may be appropriate to actually provide a mini training program that outlines for internal advocates the values of each training program and service as well as the mission, purpose, goals, and objectives of the HRD program. This will help ensure that the message is communicated properly.

5. Create a Thirty-Second Commercial. HRD practitioners must be able to communicate quickly and effectively the mission, goals, objectives, and purpose, as well as the values, of training programs and services. One way of doing so is to create a short, concise but thorough message to be communicated to interested and curious individuals within the organization—a "thirty-second commercial" about human resource development, its programs and its practitioners. This thirty-second message should include a background about human resource development, its mission, its overall goals or objectives, information about the HRD practitioners, the outcomes that HRD helps the organization realize, and the special way in which the HRD practitioners work with the organization to realize those outcomes. This is a great deal of information to get into a conversation of thirty seconds; however, it is important to communicate as much of this information in as concise and memorable a manner as possible. In fact, a better strategy might be to create a series of thirty-second commercials that can be used to promote each of the previously identified topic areas, so that you can communicate the most appropriate message to whoever the audience happens to be. Keeping the message short will also help guard against information overload, which is often the Achilles' heel of promotional communications.

Thirty-second commercials such as the ones previously discussed may also be used in other promotional material such as brochures and HRD catalogs. This will enable the promotional message to be communicated in a variety of forms and fashions. The most important message to be communicated is the values of HRD and how HRD programs help the organization realize its operational outcomes. Such a message should be the centerpiece of the thirty-second commercial strategy.

6. Sell, Sell, Sell. Selling is the essence of what promotional strategy is all about. HRD practitioners are the salespersons of the HRD program. Chapter Nine was dedicated to personal selling as a part of the promotional strategy. It is essential that one grasp the concepts introduced in that chapter and begin to incorporate them into a proactive approach to enhancing the image and credibility of HRD. If HRD practitioners do not communicate the values of their programs to organization members and decision makers, nobody else in the organization will feel obliged to do so. Therefore, it is important that HRD practitioners serve as role models in the communication of the values and outcomes that HRD helps the organization realize. It is also critical that HRD practitioners begin to see themselves in a way that is of value to the organization and its mission.

Selling is not an unprofessional activity. Selling is a way of life. Everyone is selling something in order to survive. HRD practitioners must realize that they are in a battle for the limited human and financial resources of the organization. If they are to enhance the image and credibility of HRD within the organization, they must get their appropriate share of resources. HRD practitioners must be the ones who act as advocates for the HRD program. If they do not, it is highly probable that during periods of organizational and economic decline the HRD program will be the first to be eliminated.

Step 16: Create Appropriate Follow-up Procedures for Training Programs and Services

The last action step that HRD practitioners should engage in is the creation of appropriate follow-up procedures for training programs and services. This is a way of demonstrating the responsiveness of HRD programs to organization and client needs. It is also a way of demonstrating how HRD practitioners can help the organization realize its operational goals and objectives.

Figure 10.3 reveals the amount of information that is extinguished shortly after a traditional training program. Within two

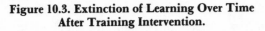

**Figure 10.3. Extinction of Learning Over Time
After Training Intervention.**

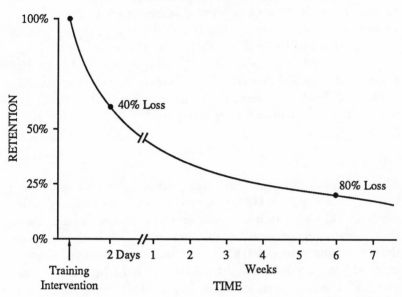

days, the typical learner has extinguished somewhere between 15 percent and 40 percent of the information acquired during the training intervention. Within six weeks after the intervention as much as 40 percent to 80 percent of the information has been extinguished. Follow-up procedures are therefore designed to help learners retain information in far greater amounts. In addition, follow-up procedures allow for rehearsal as well as practice in acquiring knowledge and developing skills. This is another way in which they enhance the probability of behavior changes occurring as a result of training interventions.

Follow-up procedures are critical if HRD clients' performance is to improve and their developmental needs are to be satisfied. HRD practitioners should become partners with clients for both purposes. If this type of relationship can be realized in an organization, clients who are served will become internal advocates who can positively communicate to others in the organization the values of human resource development.

Finally, follow-up procedures are a way of communicating

the sophistication as well as the complexities of HRD programs. This is an extremely important message to get across to organizational leaders. Only when this message is communicated, in fact, will organizational leaders and decision makers begin to advocate that professionalized HRD practitioners are essential in today's organizations. Only when decision makers and organizational leaders realize that HRD is sophisticated, complex, and valuable will HRD be perceived as an equal partner with other operational units within the organization.

Conclusion

The creation of a strategic marketing planning process is both complex and complicated. HRD practitioners have the abilities to develop the kinds of training programs and services that make a difference in an organization. But they often fail to communicate the virtues and values of HRD to key decision makers and organizational leaders. For too long they have allowed others in the organization to communicate value and importance to the organization. HRD practitioners must empower themselves and become proactive in their assertion that HRD is a valuable and critical component in today's organization.

For the past several decades various resources within organizations have come to the forefront during periods of economic growth and recovery. During the early part of this century, physical resources were used to enhance competitiveness and profitability. During the past twenty years, our financial resources have been viewed as vital to competitiveness and profitability. During the next several decades, human resources will become the leverage point for organizations in terms of their competitiveness, their profitability, their effectiveness, and their efficiency. If organizations are to be competitive in the year 2000 and beyond, those in charge of HRD must become equal partners with other operational leaders. In order for this to become a reality, HRD practitioners must become passionate about improving the credibility of HRD programs. The authors hope that this book will, in a small way, help to enhance the image of HRD.

References

Barich, H., and Kotler, P. "A Framework for Image Management." *Sloan Management Review*, Winter 1991, pp. 94–104.

Barker, L. L. *Communication*. Englewood Cliffs, N.J.: Prentice-Hall, 1981.

Barry, T. E. *Marketing: An Integrated Approach*. Chicago: Dryden Press, 1986.

Brinkerhoff, R. O. *Achieving Results from Training: How to Evaluate Human Resource Development to Strengthen Programs and Increase Impact*. San Francisco: Jossey-Bass, 1987.

Clark, J. *Business Today: Successes and Failures*. New York: Random House, 1979.

Engel, J. F., and Blackwell, R. D. *Consumer Behavior*. Chicago: Dryden Press, 1982.

Ferrell, O. C., and Pride, W. M. *Fundamentals of Marketing*. Boston: Houghton Mifflin, 1982.

Gilley, J. W. "Practical Tools for Developing a Comprehensive Training Strategy." *Lifelong Learning: An Omnibus of Practice and Research*, 1987, 10(6), 10–16.

Gilley, J. W. "Marketing Your Professional Certification Program." *Association Management*, Nov. 1988, pp. 111–113.

Gilley, J. W. "How to Collect Data." *INFO-LINE*, no. 9008. Alexandria, Va.: American Society for Training and Development, 1990.

Gilley, J. W., and Eggland, S. A. "Hook, Line and Sinker." *Training and Development Journal*, 1987, 41(9), 22–29.

Gilley, J. W., and Eggland, S. A. *Principles of Human Resource Development*. San Diego, Calif., and Reading, Mass.: University Associates and Addison-Wesley, 1989.

Gilley, J. W., and Moore, H. A. "Managers or Career Enhancers?" *Personnel Administrator*, 1986, 31(3), 51–59.

Gordon, J. "The First Thing Cut?" *Training*, 1987, 24(11), 43–50.

Kotler, P. *Marketing for Nonprofit Organizations*. (3rd ed.) Englewood Cliffs, N.J.: Prentice-Hall, 1986.

Kotler, P. *Marketing Management: Analysis, Planning and Control*. (2nd ed.) Englewood Cliffs, N.J.: Prentice-Hall, 1987.

Kotler, P., Andreasen, A. R. *Strategic Marketing for Nonprofit Organizations*. Englewood Cliffs, N.J.: Prentice-Hall, 1987.

Livitt, T. "Marketing When Things Change." *Harvard Business Review*, 1977, 55, 107–113.

Lovelock, C. H., and Weinberg, C. B. *Marketing for Public and Nonprofit Managers*. New York: Wiley 1984.

McCarthy, E. J., and Perreault, W. D. *Basic Marketing: A Managerial Approach*. Homewood, Ill.: Irwin, 1984.

Martelli, J. T., and Mathern, D. "Statistics for HRD Practice." *INFO-LINE*, no. 9101. Alexandria, Va.: American Society for Training and Development, 1991.

Olivetti, L. J. (ed.) *ASTD Trainer's Toolkit: Mission Statement for HRD*. Alexandria, Va.: American Society for Training and Development, 1990.

Peter, J. P., Donnelly, J. H., Jr., and Tarpey, L. X. *A Preface to Marketing Management*. Plano, Tex.: Business Publications, 1982.

Peters, T. J., and Waterman, R. H. *In Search of Excellence: Lessons from America's Best-Run Companies*. New York: Harper-Collins, 1982.

Rackham, N. *SPIN Selling*. New York: McGraw-Hill, 1988.

Robinson, D. G., and Robinson, J. C. *Training for Impact: How to Link Training to Business Needs and Measure the Results*. San Francisco: Jossey-Bass, 1989.

Rogers, C. R. *On Becoming a Person*. Boston: Houghton Mifflin, 1961.

Rogers, E. M. *Diffusion of Innovations.* (3rd ed.) New York: Free Press, 1983. (Originally published 1962.)

Swan, J. E., and Combs, L. J. "Product Performance and Consumer Satisfaction: A New Concept." *Journal of Marketing Research,* Apr. 1976, pp. 25–33.

Warmke, R. F., and Palmer, G. D. *Principles of Marketing.* Cincinnati: South-Western Publishing, 1985.

Index